Hilary Townsend was born into a Blackmore Vale farming family, spending her early childhood at Hewletts Farm and Thornhill, before moving to Stalbridge. She became a personnel manager in industry, then a lecturer in management subjects at Frome Technical College, while writing about Dorset as a hobby. Made redundant when the college closed, she was able, after years of homesickness, to return to the Blackmore Vale and write full time. A passionate conservationist who has spent many years restoring her medieval house in Stalbridge, she now writes about this work, especially for North American publications. She has made broadcasts for the BBC on her childhood, Thomas Hardy's parlourmaid, and William Barnes, is well-known as a lecturer on the Blackmore Vale and its traditions, and is the author of 'Discover Dorset' *Blackmore Vale* (2004).

BLACKMORE VALE CHILDHOOD

Home Remembered

Hilary Townsend

THE DOVECOTE PRESS

To my parents and Mary with love

ACKNOWLEDGEMENTS
I am grateful to Mary's children and Jennie for reading the
manuscript, and I would like to record my special thanks to my
computer teacher Leslie Tanner, without whose patient guidance I
might still be using a dipper pen.

First published in 2006 by The Dovecote Press Ltd
Stanbridge, Wimborne Minster, Dorset BH21 4JD

ISBN I 904349 50 I

© Hilary Townsend 2006

Designed and produced by The Dovecote Press Ltd
Printed and bound by Biddles Ltd, King's Lynn, Norfolk

A CIP catalogue record of this book is
available from the British Library

1 3 5 7 9 8 6 4 2

Contents

I

A Beautiful Place

WE LOVED the farm. It was a dairy farm called Hewletts
deep in Dorset's Blackmore Vale, a few fields from the
River Stour, the 'cloty Stour' beloved of William Barnes. In
summer, mowing grass full of clover and moon daisies grew
waist high and, in the autumn rains, the cows stumbled to the
yard stogged in heavy Oxford clay.

We loved the farmhouse too. A handsome house of stout
Portland stone, square, like a child's drawing of a house, it had
a flagged, walled courtyard to one side between the kitchen and
the farmyard. Into this courtyard a man came every morning,
turned a sneck up on the tall, iron water pump and pumped a
hundred strokes to fill the water tank in the attic. Beyond the
courtyard on the other side of the kitchen wall was the dairy. It
was purpose-built and of course on the north side of the old
house. Thick walls and small windows gave the dairy a dim,
mysterious look while the cold smooth old flagstone floor,
combined with fresh, unpasteurised milk and milk churns,
produced a distinctive smell I have never met anywhere else.

In 1920, when he bought the farm, my father planted a row
of cypress trees beside the lawn in the shelter of the old, raised,
wooden granary, where they flourished. Then my mother
planted snowdrops at their base and by this means I got my
very first impressions of the world – the smell of the cypress as
I sat in my pram, and the excitement in early February every
year of leaving the breakfast table and running out with my
sister to see if any snowdrops were out. 'Please God' I would
pray as we ran. 'Please let them be out.' By this means I got my

first experience of religion too and, if they were out, of prayers being answered.

The farm was isolated – two miles from the village and at the end of a long lane – so the stock became personalities and, sometimes, friends. I soon learned that when the fat sow who lived in the orchard had a litter (which was often) she was 'funny', i.e. cantankerous and better avoided, but the horses never had moods.

Tom, my very favourite, was a sturdy Welsh cob who had seen service in the Great War – indeed, my father had bought him at a sale of cavalry horses. He gave us years of faithful service in a dependable routine – we always felt he must have been glad to be out of the fighting and earning his living on a peaceful Dorset farm.

Much of Tom's life was spent pulling loads in carts on the farm, but when he could be spared he was harnessed into the trap and my mother would drive us to the village. I loved the trap and our outings in it. I noticed the sound of the wheels scrunching on the road when we turned off the stony farm track and on to the gravelled highway, and I loved the wide band of smooth wood all round the top of the body, like a running board but at hand height – perfect for drumming little fingers on.

Our other horse was a strong, dark brown waggon horse known as Chink.

'Why is he called Chink?' I asked my father one day, looking at the horse's broad, gleaming, brown back.

'His real name is Captain' he replied. 'But when he was young he 'chinked back' into a hay rake.' He had injured himself, always walking with a very slight limp afterwards, though his accident did not seem to have affected him and the name Chink stuck.

Our herd of dairy cows was an assortment of colours and sizes, as cows were in those days. It was to be many years before they all became uniform black and white in the

Blackmore Vale, so that it looked as if the fields were playing dominoes.

The heavy clay ground, well watered by the River Stour, meant dairy farming for it was much too wet for sheep. And pigs, which need to lie dry, were not really suited to it either.

In any case, my father did not like pigs, ever since one hot summer's day when the postman cycled down from the village. Taking his coat off and slinging it across the carrier, he leaned his bicycle against the orchard fence while he took the letters through the garden to the house. When he returned, the old sow in the orchard had found the sleeve of his jacket hanging down on her side of the fence. She was of an adventurous and determined nature so she had eaten the sleeve. The Post Office demanded payment for a new jacket and, although my father protested that a postman who couldn't see a sow and ten piglets in the orchard shouldn't be on the road, he still had to pay for it.

The heavy clay soil so near the river became a sea of mud in the winter, but in the spring and summer, oh, we had our reward then, for the rich dairy pasture gave us glorious wild flowers. Celandines first, then violets, white and sweetly scented, sheltering under their dark green leaves. You really had to search for them. Mauve violets, not so highly scented and much more outgoing, were more easily found, and dog violets (pale mauve, big and with no scent at all) seemed to put themselves about everywhere. Then primroses, especially by the streams and wherever moss grew.

Next came cowslips, fat and long stemmed, scented and plentiful in the Home Ground of the farm and all along the railway line banks, for the line ran through our ground. And I remember the excitement when a much rarer oxslip was found. Bluebells followed, a carpet of purest blue seen from the drive of Thornhill House, the house the famous painter had built for himself when he made a fortune from his paintings, or in the old woods around the village in patches among the green dog's mercury. I've always loved blue and green together ever since. Cuckoo flowers, sometimes called lady's smock, followed the bluebells, then ragged robin in the hedges and moon daisies at midsummer in the mowing grass – we took them all so much for granted.

My father was a quiet man, some years older than my mother, and farming, which he loved, was the only life he knew. He and my mother had married in 1920 and my sister Mary was born the following year. She was born at home at Hewletts Farm but several miscarriages followed her birth, one of them rather serious, so when I came along it was arranged that I should be born at The Old Malt House at Sturminster Newton, the local maternity home six miles away. I was always a bit sorry about that. I should so much rather have been born in the sturdy old farm house with all the sounds and sights of farm life around me. And anyway, Sturminster Newton is such a lot to get into the little line marked 'place of birth' on passport and visa forms.

To reach lonely Hewletts Farm you turned off the gravelled road from the village on to a farm track to Bungays Farm. Then you turned right down our own, often rutted, lane with a wide strip of grass growing up between the tracks made by generations of carts and waggons. Then we had to cross the railway line, the single track of the Somerset and Dorset Joint Railway that ran from Bath down to Bournemouth. This entailed opening the heavy railway gates on both sides of the single track (and shutting them again carefully) before going the last lap to the farm.

The isolation was reduced by delivery vans – Dikes, the village baker and grocer, regularly delivered our orders, rattling down the lane in their own firmly labelled Ford van. And, of course, commercial travellers came to see my father. One of these represented an old established cattle feed firm named Bibbys. It was a name I repeated to myself over and over, 'Bibbys, Bibbys,' until it became almost romantic.

A domestic help named Beatty came down to the farm on certain days. I think she rode back with my father and Tom after he had taken the churns of milk up to the milk factory in the village, or she cycled, or put her bike in the cart and then cycled home. Sometimes, too, my parents felt able to extend to a live-in help, though, from tales that came down to me later, these experiments were not always successful.

Our closest friends were the family at Bungays Farm, the next farm to us along the lane. Mr. and Mrs. Day had a daughter named Nancy who was a bit younger than my sister Mary but the two became firm, almost inseparable friends, a friendship which endured steadily throughout their lives.

The farm track was so little used that it was regarded as safe and as soon as Mary was considered reliable in the matter of closing the railway line gates, she could visit our neighbours on her own. Sometimes I was allowed to go with her and I loved these visits. Mrs. Day had the most beautiful, deep, well modulated speaking voice. Every word she spoke sounded exciting and unusual and I longed, almost prayed, that she would not stop speaking.

Nancy had a doll named Victoria, a beautiful big china doll with lovely clothes, well groomed hair, a delicate pink and white complexion and big mysterious eyes – all the things I envied most and wished for my four year old self. I never touched Victoria and was certainly invited to pick her up. She remained a sort of goddess and when the time came to go home, I was glad that there were drab brown ducks on the duck pond near the front door. They were clumsy and ungainly on land and noisily gobbled up duck weed in the water, as ducks should. I was really relieved to see them – they brought me down to earth.

My mother, who loved people and enjoyed cooking, decided that in the summer she would take paying guests. She had some cards printed which said firmly 'board residence'. I do not know where she advertised but the work brought her a series of interesting visitors to that remote farm house. Sometimes families with several children came and, once, a nanny brought a little boy in need of country air. Nanny became a firm friend and kept in touch with us after the holiday. I remember thinking that Nanny was a lovely name for a grown up. It was a great disappointment when a few years later she came to see us and I learned that her name was really Margery Painter.

Once a family named Taylor came to stay. Captain Taylor brought with him a wireless – the first my parents had ever heard. They were fascinated. One day, my mother told me years later, they heard a man with a hoarse voice ranting away in German.

'Who's that?' my mother asked him.

'Oh, just another rabble rouser,' replied the captain. 'You get them all over Europe. He'll shout for a bit then vanish. Name of Hitler.'

My mother's relations often came to stay. Her mother whom she adored had died when my mother was only twenty, leaving her to look after her somewhat curmudgeonly father and two younger sisters. The elder of her sisters, Pat, made a wartime marriage to a soldier in 1917 but the marriage did not survive and their son Dick, who was the same age as Mary, was sent to boarding school and spent his holidays with us.

The younger sister, Millie, had been only nine when their mother died so she was always extremely close to my mother, who had virtually brought her up. Auntie Millie, dark, vivacious and extremely beautiful was our favourite aunt and we loved the way heads turned to look at her when we were out together. She was only eighteen years older than Mary, they were almost like sisters.

In the early 1920's my mother's father, a widower for some ten years, announced that he was going to marry again. My mother was taken aback by this news. She had loved her own mother so much and might not be able to accept a stepmother. What, for a start, should she call her? She need not have worried. The new wife, a gentle, soft-voiced widow was a perfectly sweet elderly lady and my mother became sincerely attached to her. The happy couple spent their honeymoon at the farm. Mary, who was a small child running about by then, called her 'Grandma', so my mother realized that she too could quite properly call her 'Grandma' too and that problem was solved.

My grandfather's honeymoon brought another and unexpected advantage to my parents. My grandfather was an enthusiastic and accomplished wood worker. He saw at once that what the farm needed was a stout farm gate into the yard from the lane. I believe he also made the sturdy rails above the row of flag stones on end that edged the garden. All his work was first class and the farm gate, made of oak, was still there many years after we were gone from the scene.

We were gone from the scene when I was four years old. The agricultural depression which was such a feature of the 1930's had made my parents' life increasingly difficult and my father, over fifty and never particularly robust, could not cope with it. We moved from Hewletts Farm to a small holding at Thornhill about two miles away and lived in a cottage there belonging to my father's aunt, the redoubtable Aunt Em.

Thornhill is a hamlet a mile and a half from the village of Stalbridge, and living there we were within sight of Cooks Farm, my father's boyhood home.

My father's family had farmed in the Blackmore Vale within a few miles of Stalbridge for generations. My great grandfather George Rabbetts, born in 1795 at Gillingham, farmed at West Stour and finally at the Manor Farm, Bagber, at the Stalbridge end of the beautiful halter path to Sturminster Newton. Bagber is a hamlet about three miles from Stalbridge and very near the River Stour. Old George had a busy life there. He was a hard working yeoman farmer, a magistrate at Sturminster Newton and a member of the Board of Guardians who oversaw the workhouse there. Then there was the chapel. The family were

Congregationalists and I have no doubt that his forebears had come out in support of Cromwell some hundred and fifty years before his birth, but there was no Congregational Chapel at Sturminster Newton. The nearest was in Stalbridge so old George faithfully attended Chapel services there. He probably drove along the country lanes in the high wheeled gig of the mid-nineteenth century, to join the growing congregation of Independent worshippers at Stalbridge.

The only photograph we have of him, taken in the very early days of photography, shows a jovial looking white haired old man with light coloured side buttoned leggings over light trousers, black waistcoat and long black jacket, and on the prim little table beside him a tall black hat. Old George married twice and his second family was a replica of the first, each producing a daughter and two sons.

His first marriage to Elizabeth Morgan in 1817 produced a daughter Rachel and sons Charles and William. His second marriage to Hester Morris in 1848 produced a daughter Ann and sons Henry (my grandfather, born in 1849), and George born four years later. These three were the children of his middle age and he was obviously devoted to them, describing them in his will as 'My three dear children'. Both his marriages had been by licence and it had been assumed for some time that the reason for this was the imminent arrival of the first child. However, examination of the marriage and birth certificates shows that this was not so. The more likely explanation is that George, a devout Non-conformist, was obliged to be married in his parish church, to which he did not subscribe. If his marriage could be by licence, then he would not have to have his banns read and his name called in Church for three successive Sundays, a situation he would seem to have preferred.

When Old George died he was buried at Stalbridge in the tiny scrap of graveyard beside the newly consecrated Congregational Chapel in Station Road. That was in 1872 and a few years later Hester was buried beside him. I suppose my great grandparents were honoured by being buried in the very small graveyard because they were generous and hard workers in the chapel.

After Old George's death, my grandfather Henry managed the Manor Farm at Bagber. Henry was only 23 at the time of his father's death and by all accounts he was rather a wild young man who kept company with some dare-devil young companions. He and later his brother George joined the Dorset Yeomanry, a territorial unit that had been founded in 1794 to strengthen the Militia because of the threat of invasion by Napoleon and the French armies across the Channel. The Yeomanry were under canvas for a few weeks every year and as the Yeomen were required to provide their own horses, the camp would have been full of young farmers with some independent means. They were also renowned for their love of dressing up and a picture that has come down to us Great Uncle George in his uniform seems to bear this out. Fortunately for my family Henry forsook his former ways and friends and became a staunch supporter of the Chapel.

Eventually Henry acquired a wife and three young children. His father George had turned the milk, which did not keep, into cheese at the farmhouse, so, sometime in the 1870's, they had engaged two young cheesemakers, sisters Maria and Emma Gunning, farmer's daughters from Glastonbury. The girls had packed up their clothes in a black wooden brass studded trunk (we still have it) and laid their ribbons and scarves in the tray at the top.

Possibly the railway, or more probably the carrier's cart, brought the two young girls and their black trunk to Bagber Manor Farm to make cheese. Henry married Maria in 1879 and her sister Emma stayed on with them for the rest of her life. Aunt Em was as strong as a horse and an excellent cheesemaker.

Henry decided that as soon as the tenancy of a suitable farm fell vacant he would leave the Manor Farm to his brother to run. In 1884 a suitable vacancy occurred and Henry moved his family to Cooks Farm at Thornhill, a good country mile outside Stalbridge. At Thornhill in the seventeenth century Sir James Thornhill, the painter of the dome of St. Pauls and father-in-law of Hogarth, had built himself an impressive mansion. Cooks Farm, across the fields from this remarkable house was a beautiful, sturdy Portland stone and slate farmhouse. It had been rebuilt in the 1860's by the Stalbridge Estate as a 'handsome residence' though a Cook's Farm was first recorded on that spot in 1330, when farmland was reclaimed from the deep woods and forests around, and it was felt safe to settle there outside the village. Old Cooks Farm had been such an exceptionally sturdy building with wide stone walls and a stone roof that it had been hard indeed to pull down. However the Estate builders made so thorough a job of the demolition that no trace of it remains. Its successor is lovely though, handsome and well-built.

My grandfather drove his herd of cows the three miles of country lanes from Bagber to Cooks Farm with his eldest son, five-year-old Frank, trudging beside him. The people who lived at Cooks Farm before, the first tenants of the rebuilt house, had planted the garden and orchards, adding a beautiful pear tree on the south wall. The hedges had grown tall, making the lawns sheltered and warm and secluded from the road.

The cottage within sight of Cooks Farm that we now went to live in had been acquired after Henry Rabbetts' death by his widow Maria and her sister Aunt Em. Maria, my grandmother, had died in 1932 so Aunt Em lived alone until we came, and my father took over the smallholding there. Aunt Em fascinated me. She was a stout, sallow faced woman in her seventies whose many years in the manual labour of cheesemaking had given her immensely sturdy forearms. All the same, she could do beautiful sewing when, as my mother put it, 'she had a mind to' and when I ripped my dolls' clothes she mended them exquisitely.

There were no amenities in the cottage at Thornhill. Water was drawn from a well by the simple process of letting a bucket down on a chain, and the cottage was lit by candles or oil lamps. I loved it when the big brass oil lamp with its glass chimney and ornamental globe was brought into the sitting room on a winter's afternoon. The curtains were drawn, the fire was lit and I was allowed to bring it up with the bellows – big, fat, red leather bellows that sighed over their work.

Oil lamps were used in the downstairs room. To go to bed we used candles in wide candlesticks of enamel or pewter, with a box of matches permanently resting in them. This was most important as a sudden draught could blow the candle out, leaving nothing but inky darkness and shaking fingers. Fire was a hazard of course, and I was not allowed charge of my own candle until I was eight years old.

When I was small, undressing and washing took place downstairs by the kitchen range in winter before I was put to bed. Saturday night meant a bath in the brown tin hip bath that stood before the fire on the rag rug. The rag rug was always there. My mother, who was clever with her fingers, had made it many years before, using scraps of worsted material which had originally come from samples of men's suiting. These strips of material, black and dark grey, and occasionally scarlet, were pegged through a hearth rug sized piece of canvas, and showed on the front in even, semi-circular pieces. The back was covered with hessian. The whole made a thick, warm, serviceable rug and a bath mat for small feet.

At bedtime, as long as it was cold, my mother carried me upstairs close to her, so that the draughts didn't notice. Then into bed, feet tucked up tight in a long winceyette nightdress until the bed got warm enough to move them down a bit and stretch out.

Prayers were said in bed on such nights, my hands folded, and my eyes not too firmly closed, as I asked God to bless all the members of the family and make me a good girl. We would talk for a bit in the candlelight, my mother and I, she never seemed to be in any hurry at bed time. Then she would kiss me goodnight and go downstairs, taking the candle with her. I was never offered a night light of my own, so I suppose it did not occur to me to expect one. Sometimes, if the moon was bright the curtains would be drawn back and the light flooded the little bedroom I shared with my sister.

One night the full moon, a bright yellow harvest moon, seemed to call me with its brightness and I got up and knelt on the window seat, gazing at it. Mary came in. 'What's the moon made of, Mame?' I asked her. 'Green cheese,' she replied with convincing promptness. I marvelled at this piece of news, the last thing I expected. Then I said gravely. 'Yes, it's cheese shaped isn't it, but it's not really green. I heard my sister laugh delightedly. It wasn't true. The moon wasn't made of green cheese at all. I'd believed her and now she was laughing at me.

The laughter stopped suddenly though, for I hurled myself bodily off the window seat, feet and elbows flying, kicking and screaming with fury, and completely winded her. Poor Mary. She may have been thirteen years old to my five, but I had the advantage of surprise and I really hurt her. The curious thing was, though, that once my mother had arrived and the noise and explanation of this scene were over, I never did discover what the moon was made of.

The only real variation of the bedtime routine came suddenly, when my mother became ill. She had grazed her leg against the ancient metal bucket she used for the hens' meals and scraps. It went septic and complete rest was ordered. This meant that I was put to bed beside her in the big bed with a brass rail at either end, and a deep soft feather bed to lie on.

My mother would read to me or, better still, tell me stories of her own making, then kiss me goodnight and, as I grew drowsy beside her, I waited for the next unvarying sequence of events. She would turn over to face the candle, pick up her book from the floor and start to read. Perfect quiet and stillness followed. Then, a few minutes later, she would start to laugh, shaking with silent laughter caused by reading novels by someone she had told me was called Victor Bridges.

My mother had a terrific sense of humour and would rock and shake with laughter, pause, grope under the pillow for a handkerchief to mop her streaming eyes, then shake with laughter again. I lay beside her pretending to be asleep but all the time, as we both shook and rocked in the big bed, I imagined I was in a ship on a rough sea or about to be swallowed by a whale, like Jonah. I had started Sunday School at the little mission house at Poolstown so I knew about such things. Perhaps I'd be shipwrecked like Robinson Crusoe or cast over the side to do some tremendous act of bravery like the little cabin boy in the song 'The Golden Vanity'. No, on second thoughts I wouldn't be him because his shipmates went back on the bargain they made and left him to drift in the lowland sea.

I knew all about the little cabin boy of the Golden Vanity because Mary used to sing it to me. She had the most lovely singing voice and sometimes in the evening, when the noisy boys who were her usual companions had gone home, she would come up to the room we shared and, instead of teasing me about green cheese, sing all those old ballads right through. I especially love the Golden Vanity for all its doleful tune and miserable fate. Eventually, in a lovely haze of laughter and make believe, I drifted off to sleep and when, much later, I was picked up and carried back to my own cold bed, I knew nothing whatever about it.

I was always thankful for the amount of music in our lives and we were lucky to have it. Aunt Em was driven by a sour, narrow religion. The wireless, she told us, was the devil's works. Anything one might enjoy seemed to her to be devil's works, and she did not lose an opportunity to read us improving tracts and dwell on sin and death. My high spirited sister had her own methods of dealing with all this. She turned the dreary framed texts to face the wall. Then there was the time when the boy from the cottage next door came in and the two were sitting quietly in the kitchen and Aunt Em insisted on reading a long tract about sin and damnation to them. Mary dealt with that too by nudging the boy and signalling climbing out of the open window. They did it so noiselessly that Aunt Em went on reading for some time and had no idea that her audience had vanished.

Aunt Em and my grandmother and their large family of brothers and sisters had been brought up in Glastonbury as members of a sect known as The Plymouth Brethren, a Calvinist sect that feared contamination by the world and its sinful ways if they were exposed to them. It was, I learned much later, a sect that stressed the Word of God but not the Love of God, whose God could be easily offended and stoop to terrible revenge.

There was, however, a piano in the cottage at Thornhill. Obviously that had not been regarded as devil's works, at any rate as long as it was used to play hymns and sacred music, of which there was an abundance around the instrument. A hymn book, no doubt Sankey and Moody, was permanently open at 'Now the Day is Over' which I begged to be allowed to 'play'. The result was thunderous and the whole family was glad that I soon got bored with it. My mother, however, loved music and was a good pianist. She had obtained a copy of a lovely setting of the Twenty Third Psalm called 'Brother James's Air' and she and Mary sang it, with Mary singing the descant while my mother played. They were absorbed in it one day when I had something I desperately wanted to tell my mother. I ran in, opened my mouth to speak and then the music washed over me and I stopped. In any case, I reflected sadly, they had no idea I was in the room, so I crept out again. Years later, in 1947, Princess Elizabeth chose that music for her wedding.

2

Going to School

HOME LIFE at the cottage at Thornhill was very much a private world and I was lucky to be able to spend so much time on my own. At least, I thought so, though my mother did not always agree and sometimes arranged for twins, girls of my own age, named Esme and Stella, who now lived at nearby Cooks Farm, to come over and play. They were good companions but in any argument they always, being twins, took sides with each other, whatever the rights and wrongs of the case, so in the end I was glad to be on my own again.

The other serious threat to my privacy was my sister Mary, eight years older than me, tall and energetic with a terrific sense of humour, she always seemed to prefer the company of boys. Our cousin Dick would often bring a friend from boarding school when he came to stay with us for the holidays and local boys would join them. They were all strapping well-grown adolescents and to me, as they laughed and shouted and called to each other, they seemed a race of giants. They always wanted to do complicated things. Finally, one day, they made a raft to float on the cow pond and, wondering how to test it, looked at me. I guessed their intention at once and fled indoors to my mother screaming in such tell tale terror that afterwards I was left in peace.

Peace meant the swing in the poplar tree, it meant getting in among the old laurel bushes and smelling the spicy smell of the speckly, green leaves. It meant the smell of dusty brown feathers as the hens basked in the sunshine, the creak of the well chain winding round the big roller as the water bucket came up. And at night it meant the smell of paraffin and a yellow flame in my father's newly lighted storm lantern.

Now my peace and solitude were about to be threatened much more seriously, for I was five years old and it was time to go to school. All the familiar things of home would still be there, I supposed, when I came home from school, and anyway, from what I could gather, school wasn't bad really. Mary went to school in the village and sometimes she brought home from the cookery class the most wonderful apple dumplings.

Mary also filled the house with songs she had learnt at school. The village school taught an amazingly wide range of songs – folk songs, negro spirituals, anthems, settings of the psalms and a lovely setting I've never heard anywhere else of a poem by George Herbert called 'Lord Thou hast Given me a Cell'.

It went on:

'*A little house whose humble roof is weather proof;*
Under the spars of which I lie both soft and dry.'

Oh, I knew just how George Herbert felt about that little cell. It sounded even friendlier than our garden shed or the dry little meal house where we kept the sacks of meal for the hens.

One of the folk songs was 'Swing Low, Sweet Chariot'. I particularly loved that song and Mary seemed to sing it with all the feeling in her heart. When she got to the bit that went 'I looked over Jordan and what did I see, coming for to carry me home, a Band of Angels coming forth to me, coming for to carry me home,' I could see all this quite clearly. I looked across to the big field sloping up hill towards the North Lodge of Thornhill House. It was farmed by Mr. Ernie Frizzle and every June it grew waist high with mowing grass.

As Mary sang I saw the Band of Angels. They were in a chariot. It was horse drawn by fair ground style horses with flaring nostrils and was being driven down across the field of mowing grass at a furious rate. It was an untidy looking chariot and pale, hazily mauve-coloured, unconcerned angels were hanging out of it all round the sides. Then it vanished suddenly but I knew it had been a band of angels because it had skimmed lightly over the top of the mowing grass and not one stalk of grass had been bent over by its passing.

To school, then, I went at the age of five, to the Junior School at Stalbridge, in what is now called Duck Lane. It had in the nineteenth century been sometimes referred to as Farm Lane but in the nineteen thirties it had no name, it was just a lane leading to Home Farm. The School, a Church of England School, had been erected in 1871 as a consequence of the 1870 Forster Education Act and later enlarged to commemorate the 1897 Diamond Jubilee of Queen Victoria.

The Junior School was a stout stone building with thick walls and high Gothic windows. First came double doors into the porch, like a church porch only smaller, with flag stones, and there were hairy coconut mats at the two doors leading out of it into class rooms. The porch walls were lined with rows of massive Victorian coat pegs at child height, with one peg capable of holding about six wet garments for each child. The door at the end of the porch led into the infants' class, while the other door (to the right) led to one long classroom at a T junction to the infants's room. This long classroom could be partitioned into two. The classrooms had that most marvellous form of heating, a coke fired Tortoise Stove, with a cast iron tortoise in the middle of the top, and the words 'Slow but Sure' round it. Perhaps one stove for each of those high ceilinged draughty rooms was not really adequate, but we were warm enough. Our little third of a pint milk bottles, with cardboard tops and a hole for our straws, got warm too. They were tucked inside the thick wire mesh fireguard beside the stove to be warmed ready for playtime.

Cloakrooms with child-sized hardware, one for the boys and one for the girls, were across the playground in a building clearly modelled on a cowshed. All round the school lay the rambling tarmac playground edged with a high stone wall on three sides. On the fourth side, in front of the school, facing the lane, the wall was low and there were railings to look through, or to catch our chins on if we climbed them.

I started school with Miss Farthing in the infants' class. Miss Farthing was a born infant teacher with a comfortable figure, glasses and a great love of five-year-olds, no matter how messy or disagreeable. 'My babies,' she called us and she drilled us with the alphabet until we all learned to read well.

Slates were still used in the infant class in those days and slate pencils screeched on them most horribly, setting the teeth on edge. Perhaps because of this noise most of the time we used chalk, white, blue, green, yellow and a particularly throat-gripping shade of raspberry red. It was this red chalk which I always seemed, everyday, to get all over the front of my dress and across my face

We went to school in the morning in the back of a shooting brake from Thornhill House. The owner of the Thornhill Estate, the greatly respected Major Wynne-Jones, sent his chauffeur up to the village every morning for supplies so that the Thornhill children, Esme and Stella, the twins from Cooks Farm, their two sisters and several other children besides me from isolated farms, could get a lift to school. It was an act of kindness for which I could never be thankful enough, for I always found the long walk home on my five-year-old legs very tiring.

Our lift every morning meant that we arrived at school in good time for register and prayers. As it was a Church of England school, prayers and hymns began the school day and simple prayers ended it. We were taught to put our hands together and close our eyes tight. I closed mine so tight that blobs and patches of yellow light passed across my shuttered eyeballs with such fascination that they quite took my mind off the prayers.

I knew, I suppose we all did, that Miss Farthing loved us. We really were her babies, all the assorted and often grubby crowd of us. I never remember her raising her voice or punishing anyone, and her patience was endless. She was shortsighted and, even with thick glasses, did not seem to see well at any distance. I think this meant that her only reality was nearby, so she filled her life cheerfully and exclusively with her dusty little school room, its sturdy wooden infant-sized tables and chairs and the beloved 'babies'. When school was over she often called together those of us who lived a long way away. She knew we would not be met at the school gates like the village infants, so if it was a warm day and we had to carry a coat or mackintosh, she would fold it carefully and place it neatly over our arms. Unfortunately, my coat was always as untidy as a rook's nest before I reached the Post Office.

Living so far from the school meant lunch time sandwiches. My mother always sent her family out on an excellent three course breakfast on the principle that you cannot expect to raise a good steam if you don't first stoke the boiler. The lunches she packed were always generous, so, curious and ravenous, I could hardly wait to get to twelve o'clock and start on them. We were sent up the lane and along the High Street to the Parish Room, a long draughty building beside the Rectory. Here we sat on long benches facing each other to eat our lunch.

One day as I was wolfing my sandwiches with the ineffective aid of a loose front tooth, I leaned back into the gangway to look at a latecomer. The accidental blow my face received as the burly latecomer went to his place was enough to displace my tooth and make my gum bleed, so I was led out of the Parish Room and across to the scullery of the Rectory.

Here the two maids Lucy and Lily were doing the washing. The big copper was on, the huge old mangle set up, steam everywhere, and both girls were standing at large zinc wash tubs up to their elbows in soapsuds. Lucy and Lily, who were sisters, were stout, well-grown village girls and everything in the Rectory scullery that day seemed to be on a grand scale. Lily dried her sturdy forearms on a huge roller towel, then fished in my mouth with surprising gentleness. She found the tooth, washed it and gave it to me to keep. She gently washed my face and wiped away the traces of blood. Then she said quietly 'You can go back to your dinner now' and she went back to her rampant soapsuds. I was bitterly disappointed. I would so much rather have stood at the wash tub with Lily, sinking my arms beside hers into the suds.

School started again at 1.30 and the infants' afternoons often included something fairly restful, such as being read aloud to by Miss Farthing, or reading aloud ourselves to her, a chubby finger under the line of bold black print, and many an anxious pause.

Quite one of the best things about going to school, I always felt, was learning to read. I was fascinated by it from the start and as my delight showed on my face, I was constantly given and lent books. Sometimes too, I could persuade other people besides Miss Farthing to read to me. My mother was particularly co-operative about this, and in the evenings after tea she could always be encouraged to read from the Adventures of George the Puppy, or The Arkubs Annual or (my favourite of all) Tinker Tailor by Eric Vredenburg, illustrated with the most marvellous cat drawings by Louis Wain. I have been fascinated by the cat drawings of Louis Wain ever since and have always considered these illustrations among his best work. He began by drawing cats as cats, then later on put them into human situations. Finally he insisted that he drew cats as humans because that was how he saw them, but the wonderful thing about them is that they are drawn as the human beings *of his time*.

I went to bed early, we all did. We needed a lot of sleep. Life on a small, remote farm in the 1930's was very strenuous and so much work had to be done by hand. Sometimes, after dark on a winter's evening I would go up to the big waggon house beside the cowstall and find my parents sawing wood for an order to be delivered next day. They would each have a handle of the long, heavy, double-handled saw and sway backwards and forwards absorbed in the saw's rhythm, while the light from the storm lantern on a nail above their heads cast long dancing shadows on the waggon house wall. Or I would find my mother in the long garden shed plucking poultry for Christmas orders by the light of my father's storm lantern.

We played hard too. It amazes me to think how my parents, for all their busy, hard lives, rarely missed their church and chapel activities and any social events that went with them. We children played games. The spinneys and bluebell woods, horse ponds and minnowy streams gave us plenty of scope to make up games that we would continue through season after season. Then there was the school playground for more formal games. The playground of the Junior School was covered with asphalt and perhaps it was a bit unappealing, but it was large. This meant the boys could play fast games with a leather football, with laces in it, blown up hard, or they could play even rougher games with each other, shouting and chasing and striking sparks from the nails of their boots as they ran.

So if the boys were absorbed in playing with each other, the girls too could play together and we usually went to the little playground on the left of the school porch. This was a warm sheltered spot beneath the infants' classroom windows and beside the garden plots. These tiny little plots were marked out within an edge of upended stones in a triangular flower bed. Each child had its little scrap of earth and in it we planted, weeded and generally got grubby. The seeds we planted were mostly nasturtiums and marigolds, the old-fashioned scarlet and bright orange ones. These had the great virtue of showing some signs of life above the soil fairly quickly. We were all of course in a frenzy of impatience to see how the seeds were getting on. Digging them up for a progress report on their germination was strictly forbidden.

In this little playground we were safe from the sight and sound of the horrible boys. A lot of our time at playtime was spent gossiping, of course, but when we tired of that we drifted into more formal games. Ring A Roses, said to have been played in England since the time of the Black Death, was a favourite with the infants. Then came 'Poor Sally is A-Weeping', a lovely sentimental one this. Sally sat in the middle of the ring weeping, in my case, very realistically with strangled sobs, loud sniffs and – when I got really carried away – real tears. She was, she told the ring of little girls dancing dolefully round her, weeping for a sweetheart. In the end of course she was able to choose a sweetheart from the other players, and everybody danced around happily until the chosen little girl became the next Sally.

We also played a game which we made up to the words of 'Mary, Mary Quite Contrary, How does your Garden Grow'. These words were first addressed to Queen Mary – 'Bloody Mary' – who tried to overturn the Reformation, and I have often wondered since how the news of her accession, marriage, misdeeds and death came to the village. I suppose travellers, coming through from Bristol, horsemen or pedlars, would have picked up news of the affairs of the court by word of mouth from travellers from London.

When these strangers arrived in our village bearing such tidings, no doubt our sixteenth century forebears would have turned out to greet them. Then, I feel sure, they would have gone with them to one of the ale houses in the High Street. There were several, one of which had once been called The Saracen's Head, no doubt from the time of the Crusades. Village people would have settled themselves with their pewter tankards to listen to the tales the travellers had to tell. All those tales must have been told to them a matter of yards from where we children now played in the sunshine and turned their news into games. We laughed and giggled, chanting the old rhymes in the peaceful nineteen-thirties school playground, while the nasturtium seeds we had planted in our garden plots flowered scarlet all round us.

We also played 'I sent a letter to my love and on the way I dropped it' and another ring game entwined with the words 'Lucy Lockett lost her Pocket. Kitty Fisher found it' The rhyme went on to imply that when the item was found there was nothing in it 'except the ribbon round it.' Later, much later, I learned that Lucy Lockett and Kitty Fisher were mistresses of Charles II.

We made up two sides for 'Here We Come Gathering Nuts in May', the object of which was to 'fetch away' i.e. tug and heave with all our might, to capture a member of the opposing side and to carry on like this until they were all fetched away, and we won.

Another line game was called 'The Big Ship Sails on the Allee Allee O on the Last Day of September' whose meaning I never understood till many years later. I came upon *The Lore and Language of School Children* by Iiona and Peter Opie which relates it to the opening of the Manchester Ship Canal in 1894.

When we lost interest in all these games we returned, as long as we were sure of avoiding the dreaded boys, to our old favourite 'Chain Tag'. One child chased after the rest of the group until she caught one of them. These two then joined hands and chased about until they caught another, and so on until a chain of the whole was formed.

I loved these games and the companionship of the other children. My mother was right. Naturally solitary children do need the companionship of other children, whatever they may think about it themselves at the time. So it came as a great shock when, about six months after I had started school, the experience suddenly came to an end, at least for the time being. The reason for this was that scarlet fever had broken out in the village and my mother had caught it. She was rather ill and had to be sent away to the isolation hospital at Blandford in an ambulance. I shall never forget that day. It was a lovely mild September morning and Mary and I were given baskets and sent out with instructions to pick a lot of blackberries. We walked up the field to a hedge where unfortunately, the first thing Mary spotted was a bird's nest with several little birds in it, all very dead.

'Oh look, the little birds have been deserted.' Mary said without thinking.

'What's deserted?' I wanted to know.

'It means the mother left them and went away. Perhaps something frightened her or she just didn't want to stay.'

Mary knew why we had been sent out with baskets that morning but I had no idea. We picked blackberries determinedly, then, as we heard a vehicle drive away up the lane Mary started to cry. I was astonished. She never cried yet here she was sobbing bitterly. The sight of her tears was enough for me. I started to cry in sympathy so she explained that the engine we had heard was an ambulance and it had just taken our mother away. Putting this event into words made us both go quiet. I thought of the dead baby birds deserted by their mother. I looked at the medieval hedge hanging with ripe blackberries. It seemed such an abundance of fruit when you are five years old and looking at them through floods of tears.

We came home to discover that the house had to be fumigated because of the scarlet fever. This meant that although my father could stay in it, Mary and I could not. We were to go, alone and in charge of the guard, by train to Bristol to stay with my mother's beautiful sister Auntie Millie. She had no children, just a husband, but they did have a black and white terrier called Paddy. I was not at all sure how I was going to cope with all this but everyone agreed that I could take my Teddy, an enormous friendly looking Teddy. I dressed him carefully in a long white cotton nightgown that had once belonged to me and, as we were going so far from home, I decided he had better wear knickers as well. He never wore them at home.

Bristol had trams, big noisy things that clanged along the crowded streets, and moving staircases that seemed to go at a terrifying speed. I longed for home and the fields. Even long walks with Paddy on the Downs could not make up for the home I missed so much.

We came home, Mary, Teddy and I, to find my mother at home again and much better but still not well. It was decided that she must go away to convalesce and this time I went with her. We went to Gloucester to stay with my mother's father and his second wife. We all loved my mother's stepmother. We loved her rustling elegance, her small black lace edged aprons and her gentle voice. I think she realized how much I missed school for, in the mornings after breakfast, she would draw up a low stool beside her for me to sit on and tell me stories of her own childhood in the 1860's, or she would teach me useful things like how to tie neat bows on my shoe laces.

I was really sorry to leave her, but it was wonderful to come home, to sit on the train with mounting excitement until we passed Templecombe and the engine began to puff and shriek importantly as we came down the single track across the Somerset/Dorset border. Soon we arrived at gas and oil lit Stalbridge Station, with old Tom the cob outside in the trap, shaking his harness as he waited to take us home.

Home meant back to school the next day. Miss Farthing was pleased to see me, the boys' boots still struck occasional sparks as they ran about the playground and nothing else seemed to have changed at all, except that we now had a few light wooden hoops to bowl about the yard at playtime.

Jennie, my special friend, wore her thick brown hair in four big fat ringlet curls, coaxed that way by going to bed with her curls done up in rags. Her ringlets, I noticed at once, were still as neat and bouncy and shining as ever, and I showed her how to tie neat bows.

The winter ahead meant hard work at school, Miss Farthing saw to that. Christmas came and with it a beautiful china doll for me from Bristol from Auntie Millie, then the Silver Jubilee of King George V and Queen Mary. Twenty-five years on the throne – no wonder they looked so old. We celebrated with songs and games at school and a special tea party at which the children all received a beaker to commemorate the Jubilee and a slim blue book of pictures of the reign. Then came another event, much more important to us than any Silver Jubilee. We had to 'go up'. We had to leave Miss Farthing and move on to Miss Pope's class.

Above left Great Uncle George in Dorset Yeomanry uniform.

Above right My grandfather Henry Rabbetts, who lived at Cooks Farm, near Thornhill.

Below My father and his dog Tim in 1908.

Above Cooks Farm in 1908 after my grandfather's death.

Right My mother at Quedgeley Munitions Factory, Gloucester, 1917.

Below My father in 1916, the year he met my mother.

Above My parents (centre) were married quietly in 1920.

Below Hewletts Farm, my parents' first home (from the Stalbridge Estate 1918 sale catalogue).

Above Me as a babe in arms, with my mother, my sister Mary and my cousin Dick, Hewletts Farm.

Below A Dikes van outside their bakery and grocery shop, Ring Street, Stalbridge, in the late 1920s.

Top Stalbridge High Street, showing the gas lamps, and the posts on the edge of the pavement to keep cows out of the shops.

Above Stalbridge High Street, with the Market Cross beside the Rectory garden.

Top Jennie, my dearest friend. I envied her ringlets.

Above We went to Upwey Wishing Well from Weymouth, 1938.

Left Dr. Moyle, the much-loved Stalbridge doctor throughout my childhood.

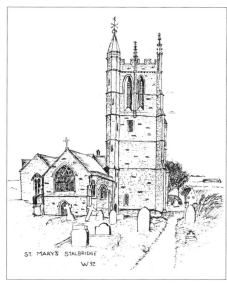

Above St Mary's Church, Stalbridge from a drawing by A.D. Wood.

Right Miss Pearse in 1966 with the then Rector, The Revd. F.A.O. Sanders.

Below With Mary and Auntie Millie in fashionable turban.

Right The Congregational Chapel 1980, little changed since 1870.

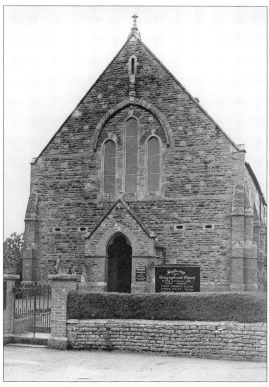

Above Mary, my mother (with teapot) and me with other children on a picnic.

Below Me with Teddy in 1940.

3
Moving to the Village

SOMETIME AFTER I had left Miss Farthing and moved up to Miss Pope's class we left Thornhill. In the hot summer days of 1936 Aunt Em was failing. She became bedridden and extremely awkward until, in the end, only Mary could do anything right in her eyes. Aunt Em died one July afternoon. Mary and Bert Dean who lived next door had heard the bell of the ice cream van and, clutching their pennies, hurried off to the main road to find it.

My mother dispatched me to find them and tell them Aunt Em was dead. They didn't believe me so we all went home and I had the satisfaction of being right.

The smallholding at Thornhill was now to have become my father's but it was found to be mortgaged to the hilt. My father, who avoided alcohol all his life and had signed the pledge at the age of sixteen, found the circumstances too dreadful to contemplate. My parents' years of care and hard work had earned them nothing and we now had to find somewhere to live. My father retired from farming and we went to live in the village in an old house in Gold Street. For all my love of the deep countryside, I was pleased about the move. For one thing, there were no more leg aching walks home after school. The Thornhill children had to walk a good country mile and a half to get home. There was no school bus in those days. We would tell stories or sing or run to one telegraph pole, then walk to the next, anything to speed up the long walk.

The old house my family went to live in now was called Snowdon House. It had once been the house and surgery of the

village Doctor and we lived in part of it. The rest was occupied
by Mrs. Gatehouse and Emily, the mother and half sister of a
girl named Dolly Gatehouse with whom my father had 'walked
out' some thirty years before. They parted and Dolly had
married somebody else. Old Mr. and Mrs. Gatehouse had been
Estate tenants of Hewletts Farm before my father bought it in
1920. I knew nothing of all this of course but I realized that my
family and Mrs. Gatehouse and Emily were well known to each
other.

Snowdon House provided the greatest possible contrast to
the cottage at Thornhill. The back of the house was much older
than the front. Mrs.Gatehouse and Emily lived in the stone
floored kitchen. Coal smouldered in a large, black grate and
the farmhouse table in the middle of the room was covered
with old black oilcloth. The house had been given an
impressive extension in the eighteenth century, giving it a fanlit
front door and a classically Georgian double front with
matching bay windows. Downstairs what had obviously been
the Georgian drawing room was still the 'best' room. Long,
low, cluttered and dim, it was made eerie by heavily
embroidered Victorian lace curtains at the window and a large
framed photograph over the fireplace of a young man in khaki.
This was Percy Gatehouse who had been killed in the Great
War.

However, Snowdon House, rambling, damp and neglected
though it undoubtedly was, had a beautiful walled garden with
patches of purple violets below the old grey walls. Halfway up
a steep hill, it gave us lovely views of the oak and elm-studded
Blackmore Vale and over it at intervals the chimes of the church
clock rang out sweetly. The chimes always played hymn tunes
and I grew to love 'Rock of Ages' and 'Abide with Me' played
in this fashion. It was this garden that inspired Mary to learn
to paint,

Best of all though for me, Jennie lived opposite in an old
farmhouse divided into two. Jennie, calm and cheerful with her

brown hair always bouncing merrily in fat and immaculate ringlets, was my dearest friend. She was an only child whose grandparents lived next door to them and who always seemed to me to have everything. Next to her family's pair of houses was an orchard full of fruit trees leading to an old farmyard. In it Jennie kept a tortoise, the first I had ever seen, and a particularly endearing buck rabbit, a handsome blue beveren named Jonathan Angus.

Johnnie Angus would come running like a puppy when called and was always pleased to see us, grunting with pleasure and flicking his whiskers against our skinny bare legs. He shared the old farmyard with a collection of fat, dusty brown hens who hated him. They had good reason to, for when in the warm afternoons the old biddies had settled down to bask in the powdery dust, and finally doze, he would run backwards and forwards among them. He kept this up until, squawking and flapping angrily, the hens were all on their feet again. That done, Jonathan Angus would hop off cheerfully and help himself to their trough of drinking water.

The village was endlessly fascinating. The triangular village green was always called The Ring because there had once been a bull ring there, and a bit beyond it was a blacksmiths' forge kept by a family who had been blacksmiths there from father to son for some six hundred years.

The High Street always seemed so busy and, for a child from a remote hamlet, it approached city life. Some heavy brown metal posts still remained along the kerb, left over from the days when such posts were all along the street. They were put there to keep cows from ambling into shops and to provide hitching posts for horses. Motor vehicles were few, mostly tradesmens' Ford vans or the Rector's or Doctor's black motor cars. Many commercial and farm vehicles were still horse drawn. Coal was delivered in thick jute sacks from a big coal waggon. The patient cart horse who drew it greatly appreciated a Cox's pippin from my flat palm as he stood stock still outside while his driver unloaded our coal.

Mr. Rattley, who baked his crusty bread behind his High Street shop, delivered it in a horse drawn purpose built bread cart with 'J Rattley, Baker' on the side. It was the delight of mischievous boys coming out of school to make tongue clicking 'Gee Up there' noises to try to make the horse go on. They did not succeed, for Mr. Rattley was never far away, but his irritation was their reward.

Milk, of course, came in a horse drawn float with a large churn fastened inside it. The milk was dipped out of the churn by a dipper with a long brass handle, half pint, pint or quart, into the customer's jug, and the dipper hung up again on the churn side. This system worked quite well as long as the milkman used proper official measures. Father's sister Auntie Kate, who had married and gone to live near London before the First World War, found herself for the first time in her life having to buy milk, and she was sure that the unscrupulous suburban milkman was cheating her. She, if anyone, knew what a pint of milk looked like and where it came up to in the milk jug. So she bought a big blue and white striped Cornish ware jug with every measure from a gill to a quart marked on the black line inside. When she presented it to the milkman next morning, the look on his face told my aunt that her worst fears about him were well founded. I still have the jug.

Hawkers and craftsmen were often about in the village street. A man came several times a year with a covered contraption mounted on a frame and powered by a bicycle, from which he ground scissors and knives. He was a quiet, pale man, despite being out in all weathers, and he always seemed grateful for any trade that came his way. The knives and scissors when returned had a wonderful edge to them and I was not allowed to touch them until they became blunt again.

Gypsies called, bearing chip baskets of stout clothes pegs they had made themselves. In the spring the gypsies brought baskets full of primroses or wild daffodils, bunches and bunches of them crammed into the deep chip baskets. There were wild flowers enough and to spare then, but my mother, who was nobody's fool, always wondered whose land they had been taken from and we did not buy them. We could in any case, always pick our own.

A lot of trade and commerce was actually carried on in the street. Two farmers, wearing leather boots and leggings, thumbs tucked into the top of cord breeches, and standing beside the cart of one of them, were no doubt driving a bargain about something. Sometimes when a catch of mackerel at Weymouth was particularly good, a cart, or occasionally a van, would appear in the village street with a man shouting 'Crow, macrow, fresh macrow.' Mother, who loved fish, took a plate from the dresser and went off eagerly in the direction of the noise. Tea, with mackerel fried and treated as only my mother knew how, was particularly delicious that day.

The shops fascinated me and my small nose was pressed to their glass more often than was good for its shape. The village was not big and the shops were typical of such a place, but they all had a definite personality. The two hairdressers, smelled exotic. The lotions they used, sweet, heavy and pungent conveyed a world of sophistication and cinema inspired glamour. The great world of grand ladies and beautiful film stars outside the village really did, I felt sure, smell like this. No doubt, too, the grand ladies all looked just like Heather Angel or Anna Sten or Jean Harlow.

Electric light was just then becoming popular. Switches were round and small and made of brown bakelite, or larger and made of brass with a thin metal switch in the middle. From my vantage point in the street I would watch fascinated as a hairdresser or shop assistant flicked the switch and the hard white light gleamed instantly all over the shop, into every cranny. It was quite different from Church where, when the gas mantles were painstakingly lit, the yellow light crept slowly down over the waiting congregation.

In our village hairdressers' shops the smell of worldly success was sometimes a bit overlaid by the reek of burnt hair. The hair got singed by hot tongs used in a marcel wave or a too enthusiastic permanent wave machine. Women who had perms had to endure a good four hours of being pulled about. Through the lighted shop windows on winter afternoons I would see their heads, heavy with ironmongery into which every strand of hair had been grimly wound, connected up to a permanent wave machine above to give the actual 'perm'. Their necks sometimes looked as if they would break under the sheer weight of metal from which they hoped to produce rows of motionless curls. At home, I reflected, we could produce motionless curls much more simply by taking my mother's old steel tongs and poking them into the fire until hot, then rolling strands of hair into them, holding the tongs still and hoping they didn't smoke, then taking out the tongs carefully and wearing a hairnet on our curls all night.

It was a relief to pass on to the sweet shop. It was a newsagents as well and here was paradise, a shop that sold sweets in long, gleaming screw-topped jars, curling twists of barley sugar and pear drops. They were big, fat, red and yellow peardrops smelling just like the nail varnish Mary had just started to experiment with. The shop sold humbugs too, fat, stripy minty humbugs, brown and white and a funny triangular shape, or fat and conventional with black and white stripes. Then there were the liquorice varieties, Spanish comfits, a sort of small, oblong shaped liquorice sweet, covered with hard sugar coating in incredibly garish colours. Or solid liquorice Pontefract cakes, quite black. Or liquorice all-sorts, yellow, orange, blue, brown and pink. And they were all crammed stickily into tall jars from which the assistant fished them out, sometimes with a scoop, sometimes with his fingers, weighed up a quarter of a pound and put them in a white paper bag which went down to a point.

Upstairs there were toys, tricycles with red wooden seats,

scarlet bonnetted pedal cars and bicycles. These were solid and heavy framed and meant to last a lifetime, which they did. The upstairs was also the bicycle showroom with a wide selection of stout steel-framed bicycles for all ages. A bicycle was a boon in those days. Many people went to work on them, morning and night, and men such as insurance agents or the Attendance Officer for Dorset schools, cycled everywhere. They often covered hundreds of miles in a month and were out in all weathers.

The District Nurse in our village did not immediately have the small car which the Nursing Association was to buy for her later, so her round had to be covered by bicycle. This meant journeys in all weathers, often down rough, muddy farm tracks.

'The sad thing about being a District Nurse' my mother once remarked 'Is that all that cycling makes their ankles so thick. It's a great shame because they do such marvellous work.'

My mother, a born nurse, would dearly love to have taken a formal training in her teens, but the early death of her own mother, leaving her with her father and two young sisters to look after made it impossible. Her comments on the nursing profession were pithy and heartfelt and I treasured them.

Bicycles had character. They needed to be maintained with love and care and a lot of paraffin. This meant the chain got soaked in paraffin every few months and the framed rubbed over with an oily rag to cheer up its appearance, while the working parts of the machine were soaked in a well-known brand of oil.

At night, of course, bicycles had by law to have lights. They had to have a reflector at the back and a small, red, battery-powered rear lamp, but it was the front light that really interested me. Many front lights were carbide lamps. They were tall and sturdy and filled with carbide (a compound of carbon with calcium carbide). And to make the carbide give a lovely white light, water was necessary. This was stored in the top of the lamp and, when it was switched on, the water dripped down slowly to form a chemical reaction and a beam of light. Carbide also had a sharp, somewhat nostril grabbing smell. I cannot describe it. I can only recognize it at once.

A carbide lamp was a lot of trouble. It had to be cleaned and provisioned for a night time journey and if the water ran out you got no light unless, of course, you had the perspicacity of two brothers who lived near Sherborne. One dark, stormy night the carbide lamp of one of them had gone out. 'Oh give it to me' said his brother and disappeared over the hedge with it. When he returned the carbide lamp threw out a lovely beam of light to guide them safely home.

If your bicycle needed maintenance beyond the skill of the owner, you took it to Vern Brown who had a small garage and cycle repair shop at the Thornhill Road end of the village. Mary once arrived with a repair to be done to her bicycle after Vern Brown had gone home for the night. She leaned the bicycle beside the front wall of the shop, hoping he would see what the trouble was. Vern saw the bicycle next day but did not touch it as he had received no instructions. Nobody else touched it either and the bicycle was there, quite safe, far several days until the matter was sorted out.

The shops in the village were generally remarkable for two things. First, they were very well stocked. Depression there may have been, but trade was trade and nobody set up in business in those days without the capital to get and keep a good stock. Next, the shops were highly specialized. With few exceptions the cobbler stuck to his last and Jack to one trade.

There was a gents' outfitters, just opposite the market cross, which stocked high class tweed jackets in quiet colours and subdued checks. Nothing here which my mother could possibly have described as 'loud', a favourite word with her. The shop was dim and quiet with that indefinable smell of good tweed and furniture polish which established at once that one was in a high class gents' outfitters. There were trilby hats, caps and deerstalkers and the well-cut tweed jackets they were worn with. There were good quality shirts too, mostly white, and plain, expensive Tootal Ties. Tootal, what a lovely name for ties. I would run down the High Street saying it over and over to myself. 'Tootal Ties, Tootal Ties'.

Another specialist shop was the jewellers and hardware shop on the corner of the High Street and Station Road. It was kept by some relations of ours by marriage and had long been established there. Old Mr. Charles Meader, the founder of the business, had trained as a watchmaker and jeweller in Blandford but the terms of his apprenticeship did not allow him to set up in business within ten miles of it. In 1873 Charles Meader and his brother considered the merits of the market town of Stalbridge and the growing resort of Bournemouth. They were offered a shop in Bournemouth but, although the pine trees were leading to the growth of sanatoria, they did not expect Bournemouth to expand east of the River Bourne. Stalbridge, however, was a bustling market town with fourteen public houses, two breweries and an excellent railway line laid a few years before from Bath to Bournemouth.

So Mr. Meader opened a shop at the top of Station Road where he sold a wide variety of goods and kept up with the times. He kept working in the shop to an advanced age, mending watches and clocks and supervising the jewellery display. Once I had to collect my father's watch, his Sunday best half hunter which had needed cleaning and regulating. ' I will see what progress has been made with it.' Mr. Meader told me gravely and went to the back room. He was rather a severe looking old man and I was impressed with his white hair and general grave demeanour. When he had gone I realized I was alone in the rambling old shop. Oh, good, an excellent time to practice my whistling. I was bad at whistling. Mary could whistle, so could all her friends. So, for that matter, could most of mine. It was a golden opportunity to see if, when I puckered up my mouth and blew hard, any sound would come. It never had before. I looked round at the empty shop. I puckered up my seven-year-old face into a perfect whistling position and I blew. The most amazing sound came out, a sharp, clear, penetrating whistle such as in London would have called up a taxi cab a quarter of a mile away. I was amazed. So was Mr. Meader. He shot back in to the shop, silver locks flying, to demand breathlessly:

'Was there something else Miss?'

'Oh no, thank you,' I replied, the very picture of innocence. 'Just my father's watch please.'

He disappeared, quickly returning to say that it was not ready and would I come back again in a week. I fled, steering my way past the calf bowls, aluminium buckets and garden tools of the hardware part of the shop.

There were two butcher's shops in the High Street, one kept by Mr. Bugg and the other by Mr. Eavis. Both butchers would stand at their shop doorways with huge carcasses of beef hanging on hooks behind them. I was terrified of them both, especially Mr. Eavis, who was immense. Both butchers did a brisk trade in tripe, bones, trotters, Bath chaps and offal, rabbits and game, as well as Sunday joints. Our house after we left Snowdon House had the sweet shop as its neighbour on the one side and Eavis the butcher on the other. 'Go next door and ask them if they've got a marrowbone, there's a good girl' my mother said suddenly one day, looking up from the morning shift of cooking in which she was happily absorbed. My mind, however, was running on things to read, so, having no idea what a marrow bone was, it seemed a good opportunity to go to the sweet shop where I could at least read all the title pages of the magazines and the headlines of the *Western Gazette*. So I went there and behind the counter the girl's face, trying not to laugh as she directed me to the butcher, was a picture.

The greengrocer's shop was a rambling old structure opposite The Hut that served as our Village Hall. The shop is now a private house but then it sold vegetables, fruit and big bottles of fizzy lemonade and ginger beer. It was kept by some people named Martin who, I always felt, especially liked my family and would let me have the biggest and juiciest apple they had (or so it seemed) for a penny.

Other shops sold groceries. There was a tiny little shop near the forge which was kept by the widow of the blacksmith Christopher Jeans. I think it sold fairly basic groceries, mostly in packets and sacks, and sweets in the ubiquitous tall glass-topped jars. The shop was dim and dark inside but I could make out fizzy, brightly-coloured bottles of Corona with a ceramic top fixed on the neck of the bottle by means of a metal cage. You pushed on the arms of this fitment and the top shot off with a most satisfying pop. We didn't buy Corona from this shop. It was delivered to our house by a merry looking Corona man who came every week.

Along the Thornhill Road there was a large corrugated iron building where a young man had boldly set up as a grocer in business on his own. He played the trumpet at the Armistice Day service every year, sounding Last Post and Reveille out over the Vale from the War Memorial in the churchyard, among the survivors who had grown up in the village with the dead. It was a moving experience. He used to call on us in the evenings after tea, to collect grocery orders, and my mother remarked afterwards that if he was prepared to put himself out like this, he would get on. His name was Charlie Jeans and after he returned from the War in 1945 he did get on.

There were other grocer's shops as well. One, called Stranges, was at the top of the lane above the Junior School. It belonged to a Mr. Strange who had another shop in Sturminster Newton, so this one was run by a Mr. Curtis. Mr. Curtis was a lively, boisterous man who, whenever I bought anything on an errand for my mother, used to bellow cheerfully:

'Have it now or take it with you?'

'I'll take it with me please,' I would murmur politely and it was some time before I worked out why my polite reply elicited such gales of laughter.

By far the largest grocer's shop in the area was Dike & Son Ltd. a family store which had been started in the High Street in 1860 by an ancestor, Henry Dike. The Dike family were justifiably proud of their baking skills and the fresh baked crusty bread of our tea had to be tasted to be believed. There were crusty, dumpy, two tiered cottage loaves which my mother always buttered, then cut with great skill into the air, not downwards on to a board.

Brown Hovis bread was another speciality of Dikes, though my mother also bought Turog bread from a baker at Henstridge. Turog had an unusual salty taste, an open texture and a lovely, rich, dark crust on top. I adored it, so did my father. One day however he had taken a bite when he realised he had a foreign body in his mouth. Carefully he fished out a large darning needle with a piece of button thread still through the eye. When the baker came again with Turog loaves in a stout, square, wicker basket, my indignant mother confronted him with:

'Mr.Cockerell, this is what my husband found in your bread.'

The baker's face lit up.

'There' he said 'And Mother's been looking for that darning needle everywhere.'

He took it gratefully and went on his way. It was one of the few times I ever saw my mother lost for words.

Dikes had many specialities besides bread. They baked cakes, hot cross buns (a dream of spice) and Easter cakes in season, or very occasionally we had a lovely chocolate Swiss roll. All the others, brightly coloured fondant covered fancy cakes, fruit and madeira cakes with thick ribbed greaseproof papers stuck firmly on to their base and sides, we did not buy. My mother had strong views on the subject.

'I simply don't understand some of the women round here, Arthur,' She would say to my father. 'They're too busy making money gloving to have time to bake, then they have to spend it buying shop cake' and she would give one of her little snorts of disapproval, and disappear into the kitchen. Tea on such a day would, I knew, be marvellous, with a freshly baked fruit cake, fat with sultanas, or little queen cakes full of fruit. On Sundays sometimes, for a real treat, we had hot, spicy Dorset apple cake.

Besides bread and cakes Dikes also specialized in home cured bacon and ham and their own sausages. They kept pigs in pigsties in Wood Lane and the meat products which were the end result really were delicious. At the back of the shop there was the bacon counter with a big, hand-operated bacon slicer. It was murderously sharp and made a sinister whirring sound back there in the shadows. The shop was tiled with typical Edwardian floor tiles, and there were sacks on the tiles full of currants or sultanas or white or brown sugar. These were weighed out by the shop assistants, every pound on the scales being put into thick blue paper bags, and marked with an indelible pencil, a tedious chore.

On the right as you entered the shop, there was the stout mahogany main counter. In the front of this at child's eye height, there were fixed, and sloping back gently, real specimens of the biscuits of a well-known biscuit manufacturer, all neatly labelled. It was a most effective presentation, designed to catch the eye, especially the greedy biscuit-eating child's eye, and it stayed there for years. The biscuits faded and slipped a bit on the slope of the display cabinet with the years, but there were still fascinating. Mrs. Dike presided over this counter. She was the daughter of a baker and grocer from Henstridge and a most capable woman. She did all the accounts, and I watched fascinated as she added up a column of figures on an account for somebody else, at the same time as she carried on a perfectly lucid and sensible conversation with my mother about her order of groceries, which was quite different. This faculty amazed me, particularly as I always struggled a bit with sums.

Mr. Dike was a short, bustling man who smelt of tobacco. He also fascinated me, but for a different reason. He always came to chapel late. I would go with my father to morning service and, as a mark of being old enough, would sit through the sermon beside father in his traditional pew. Every Sunday morning Mr. Dike would come into chapel just before the sermon. Regular as clockwork he was, bustling down the aisle to sit in his traditional pew and listen with deep attention to the sermon. I was puzzled by his organized and traditional late entry and asked my father about it. He thought for a minute then said quietly, 'Well, he's very busy with the shop, even on a Sunday. I expect the Lord knows that.' I remember being very impressed.

Besides the village people who kept shops, there were those who worked at the one factory, the milk factory. This belonged to Mr. Prideaux, the George Prideaux of the 'C and G Prideaux' on a board outside; the other one, his brother Charles, having a similar establishment at Motcombe abut seven miles away. My Aunt Kate remembered when George and his wife came to the village after they were married in 1892 with Mrs. Prideaux 'as pretty as a little doll'. Their milk factory had prospered. They lived at Grove House, where the famous Admiral Sir Charles Lambe had been born, and where there grew the biggest horse chestnut tree I have ever seen. It had taken over a large part of the garden of Grove House and hung down over the wall on to the road. Its trunk and lower branches were shored up by a foundry of iron and it only continued on its gluttonous way because, as Mr. Prideaux realized early, it was growing directly over a spring that fed Grove House's old well and garden pumps.

Prideaux's was a valued employer of men in those days and did a thriving trade in milk processing and the manufacture of Dorsella baby food. A high brick factory chimney (and its smuts) dominated Gold Street and the cold stone slabbed smell of old dairy was always noticeable as you went by. Jennie's grandfather had worked there for many years, and her uncle Bob worked there now, so we could sometimes go into the factory. We threaded our way through, with instructions to 'Look out now,' past the high stone platform where the churns were unloaded, to the cooler. This, as far as we were concerned, was the business end of the factory where the milk dripped down through a metal framed cooler into a trough at the bottom, from which it fed on to the next stage. Uncle Bob and George Hatcher would sometimes get aluminium mugs, dip them into the trough and present us both with a mug of fresh, ice cold milk. It was heaven to gulp it down on a boiling hot summer's day, in the middle of that hot and noisy factory where the men were still called to work by a steam-powered factory hooter.

Occasionally people became well known in the village through visiting it, though they did not live there. One such was a lady named Miss Cholmondeley which, my mother said, was pronounced 'Chumley'. What, I wondered, would our teachers make of that when they heard about it, as I was sure they would – from me. 'No' my mother said firmly 'Some people, though not many, have names that you spell one way and pronounce another. You just have to accept that that's what they do.'

Miss Cholmondeley came every week to take rehearsals of the Choral Society in the Parish Room, which my mother and Mary faithfully attended. The Society was well supported locally and my mother and sister loved it. They would come home after every Choral Society meeting still singing their choral parts.

A few families were not connected with trade or farming. There were not many, of course, and they tended to be the natural leaders of village society. The owner of Thornhill house, Major Wynne Jones, was regarded as the local squire by most people, though in fact he only used Thornhill for the

hunting season, retiring to his estate in Wales for the rest of the
year. A tweed clad, amiable man, much loved by people who
knew him, especially people who worked for him, Major
Wynne Jones would sometimes appear in local shops. I never
really got a good look at him, however, I didn't dare, as my
mother had impressed upon me from an early age that it was
very rude to stare. I did though form an impression of a kindly,
good natured man when he appeared at the splendid children's
Christmas party he gave every year in The Hut.

The Rector and his wife lived at the rambling Rectory (built
in 1699) in the High Street. The Rector had been a missionary
in China before his marriage and sometimes gave us a bit of
polite Chinese from the pulpit, to my great delight. They had
three pale, quiet daughters of around my own age, but I never
really got to know them. They were always either away at
boarding school or in charge of a governess. The governess was
a forbidding looking woman and in shops I used to hear her tell
the younger girls not to stare, too. So it was obviously a general
rule, Mother being, as usual, right.

One of the most well-known of village people was the doctor,
a beloved physician who finally completed more than fifty
years' service in the village. Often referred to simply as 'The
Doctor', Dr. Moyle was a man who loved obstetrics, and it was
sometimes said of him, with great pride, that 'The Doctor never
lost a baby.' This was in the days when such calamities were
not unheard of, so it was a considerable tribute. His surgery
was held at one end of his house on the very steep slope at the
top of Church Hill, towards the old part of the churchyard.

'And to get up a hill like that to see the Doctor,' my mother
would remark 'you have to be feeling well in the first place.'

The Doctor was a quiet-voiced, deeply respected man, and it
was always felt that he had the welfare of the whole village very
much at heart. At one time, it became clear that an abortionist
was operating in the area, and it was said that the Doctor,
identifying the culprit, told her that is such a thing ever

happened again, he would make a public example of her. I overhead this conversation. I was certainly not meant to hear it, so I could not ask anyone to explain to me what it meant. The result was that many years went by before I could make any sense of it.

4

Going up to the Juniors

WHEN I LEFT the infants' class I went up to Miss Pope's class. Miss Pope had a sweet face and soft voice and I thought how beautiful she was. She was also full of fascinating ideas for the class. One of these involved taking a weekly paper for six-year-olds containing a regular feature by Enid Blyton. The Blytons and their daughter Gillian seemed to have unlimited pets, cats, dogs, a pet rabbit, a pony and goodness knows what else besides. One day Miss Pope opened the paper and the letter from Enid Blyton, a regular column, contained a surprise.

'Guess what Enid Blyton has this week, children,' Miss Pope said, 'It's something quite new.' We tried to guess. We tried to think of everything. 'Another cat.' 'A puppy.' No it was neither of these. 'A long haired white rabbit,' said Jennie, who had one of her own. In the end, in a state of feverish excitement we gave up.

'It's a baby,' Miss Pope said delightedly. 'A baby sister. They are going to call her Imogen. Isn't that pretty?' The whole class was appalled. We tried to look interested. We tried, out of politeness, to share Miss Pope's enthusiasm, but a baby! A squalling, messy, demanding baby that just lay there and didn't do anything. How could anyone be pleased about that? However, Miss Pope obviously thought it was marvellous and suggested we might like to write to Enid Blyton expressing our pleasure and wishing them all well. We did. We spent several afternoons composing letters full of our polite sentiments, in pencil on lined paper. I began mine 'Dear Enid' obviously, as

she was called Enid Blyton, but Miss Pope said she was a
grown up lady and I didn't know her, so I should begin my
letter 'Dear Miss Blyton.' I rubbed out Enid and started again
but it all made rather a mess and a very grubby little offering
was put in the big envelope for Enid Blyton.

Choral singing was always a feature of our school. Miss Pope
loved singing and made us all very keen to sing, playing the
piano as we sang songs like London Bridge is Falling Down,
Shenandoah, Bobby Shafto, The Girl I Left Behind Me and The
Keel Row: sometimes we sang rounds such as London's
Burning. Finally, one day, we were put in for the County
Choral Competition. We all had to sing our very best,
breathing in the right place, sounding our words clearly and all
finishing together so that we did not sound ragged. We did this
in the presence of an adjudicator who decided afterwards that
we had done well enough to qualify for a Silver Certificate.
Miss Pope held up the certificate for the class to see. Her eyes,
I noticed, were shining.

I particularly enjoyed games lessons with her on the asphalt
covered playground. One game, called 'Crusts and Crumbs'
involved dividing us into two teams. When Miss Pope called
'Crusts' the appropriate team ran as hard as it could to touch a
marker on the wall, and when she called 'Crumbs' the other
team fled as fast as its skinny legs would take it to the opposite
wall. Sometimes her eyes would light up. She would look at us
all intently. Both teams would get ready to run their hardest
and she would call 'Christmas,' stopping us all dead in our
tracks. We thought this too funny for words.

We moved from Snowdon House to an old house in the High
Street, of three storeys with a shop in front. A long passage
beside the shop led from the front door to the dining room,
kitchen, scullery and pump room behind. The shop and dining
room made up a (probably early Georgian) frontage added to
a much older house, and we could never quite work out what
the pump room had been used for. It had a large iron pump

with a stone trough in one corner from which water was pumped up daily to a huge water storage tank in a room on the top floor. The pump room had a flagstoned floor with a drain in the middle of it and a somewhat leaky glass roof. Perhaps the floor had once been the medieval village street before our house had been built over it? Whatever its origins, it made a lovely place for growing plants and keeping my tadpoles, toad spawn and minnows in glass jam jars. It was many years before I learned that the pump room had been used by a grocer's pork butcher to salt pork and hang pigs' carcasses.

The house had many oddly shaped rooms on the two upper floors. My parents had taken it with the intention of running a boarding house, and this meant new people in our lives. Lodgings and rooms were in demand even in a remote village like Stalbridge. Sometimes people came to do temporary work, such as the steeplejack who stayed with us for two weeks while he repaired the tall brick chimney of the milk factory. Sometimes they came and stayed, like Miss Arch, a hairdresser who came up from Devon to work in the shop, let as a ladies hairdressing establishment, in the front of our house.

Miss Arch was fun. She was pretty and lively and soon she was going out with a local young farmer. One September evening after Miss Arch had gone out for a walk with her young man, she suddenly reappeared in the kitchen. She smelt of outdoors, the damp autumn night made her hair curlier than ever, and there was a sense of electric excitement all about her.

'Have you got a large basket we can borrow, please?' She asked my mother politely. 'The moon is absolutely full and Brian knows where there's a field full of mushrooms. It's quite light enough to see to pick them.'

She took the basket and was gone. I stared after her, fascinated. To be grown up and go out in the fields with one's young man picking mushrooms in the moonlight. It all sounded too exciting for words.

The only time I ever went out in the moonlight was

occasionally after tea when my father, who had been busy all day, would take advantage of its light to pick in the sweet Coxes Pippins or big Bramley cooking apples. I would beg to go with him and he would say, 'All right then, just till bedtime.' I didn't always last as long as that though because the cat would come too. Sandy, the old ginger tom, was quite sedate in daylight but on nights like this atavistic stirrings of his jungle past sent him stalking father's fingers along the apple tree's branches, then pouncing on him from the shadows cast by the fruit. Finally, my father, who did not greatly care for cats, had enough.

'Scout that cat.' He would shout. 'Take him indoors for goodness sake or we'll have this basket over.' And indoors Sandy and I would have to go.

No wonder I envied Miss Arch. Next morning on the kitchen dresser there was the basket full of mushrooms and we all, including Sandy the cat, had mushrooms and bacon for breakfast. That was how we first realized that Sandy had a passion for fried mushrooms.

'Well, they certainly spent a lot of time picking mush-rooms last night' Mother remarked to my father and they smiled at each other, a secret, nothing-to-do-with-little-girls sort of smile. Oh, I knew what they meant. Miss Arch was going to marry Brian and go down the aisle of her Devon church in a long white dress with everybody singing that hymn about the voice that breathed o'er Eden that earliest wedding day.

In fact, Miss Arch quarrelled with Brian, bitterly and finally, shortly after the night of the mushrooms, so she left the village and went back to Devon.

Two rooms in the rambling old house were taken by a retired cook housekeeper, Miss Jeans, who had been in good service. Accordingly, to my mind at any rate, she gave herself airs. She would tell my mother endless stories of the doings of the rather grand family she had worked for. She would point out to my mother how they had, on various occasions, been wise enough to listen to her advice. They had of course acquitted themselves in the world very much better as a consequence.

One August day Miss Jeans was invited to see the wedding presents given to our Doctor's daughter, a privilege not accorded to anyone else we knew. She went on about it all with such complacency and detail that for once I noticed my mother's eyes looked quite glazed.

Miss Jeans had one great redeeming feature in my eyes. She was a good cook. The two rooms she rented from us were a large bed-sitting room in the front of the house overlooking the High Street and a small narrow room behind. Here she kept a small oil stove for cooking. One of her specialities was a potted meat paste, of great delicacy of flavour and fine texture. She gave some to my mother and I was allowed to take two of Miss Jeans's potted meat paste sandwiches to school to eat at playtime. I knew how delicious they would be, and, always food loving, that was the only morning I ever found Miss Pope's lesson to drag a bit till playtime.

We seemed to become quickly established in the old house. Our big pieces of furniture saved from the farm came out of store, a great deal of shiny brown or beige linoleum got laid, and my father found work with a local farmer he had known all his life. He had abandoned the attempt to make a living by farming in 1936 because the pressures of the agricultural depression of the time proved too much for him. He had never been a particularly robust man and he was some years older than my mother.

Everything had seemed to conspire against his attempts to make a living on a smallholding which could not be diversified, and with dairy farming the price of milk was not supported. Worse still, when we moved to the village, he brought with him farm debts that he could not pay. This was a matter of particular gravity to my father, brought up on the parable of the good steward. His Liberal convictions convinced him of the rightness of free trade and a free market. All the same, his strict

Chapel upbringing and Non-Conformist conscience left him in no doubt that one day he would have to answer personally to his Maker about cow cake not paid for in 1936. He was therefore determined to repay the debts, however hard he had to work, and when eventually the last of them was repaid, it brought him a letter of thanks from the corn merchant in question that my mother cherished in her writing desk all her life. It said simply:

Dear Sir,
We beg to thank you for cheque value £11.0.0. in settlement of your account, enclosed please find stamped receipt for same.
I very much appreciate your principles in paying off this old account, and very much regret you should have had such a trying time through the years of agricultural depression; again thanking you.
Yours faithfully,
Charles Moore.

The date was a good ten years after the account had first been sent and, after so many bleak years, so understanding a letter was of great comfort to my parents. Happily, descendants of the writer are still in business in the village today.

Those years of adjustment must have been difficult for my father. Every year we still walked miles through the fields around the village, picking blackberries and wild flowers, just as we always had, but I noticed that we never went to the fields belonging to Hewletts Farm, – 'his' farm that he had taken with such delight in 1920.

My father's family had been greatly respected in the district for generations and had once been prosperous. Farming was the only thing he knew or had ever done, and he had loved it. He had brought Chink, the old cart horse, with us from Thornhill in the hope that it might be possible for him to start up in farming again one day. But Chink, put out in a rented field he did not know, fell into a deep ravine and was killed. It was a deep blow to Father's hopes. Worse still, although he was skilled at figures and had been Treasurer at the Congregational Chapel for many years, that year he was not re-elected. It hurt him very much, he told me years later, more than anything else that happened then – even more than village shops that had formerly given us credit closing our accounts. And when, to make ends meet, my father had to take work for another farmer, he must have felt that his fortunes had sunk as low as they possibly could. Yet he did not complain. His faith sustained him.

Every day was still the day that the Lord had made. He could not always rejoice and be glad in it. Indeed, on some days he could not always make out quite what the Lord had in mind for him at all, but he did not question it. Life went on and every Sunday he would get out his best suit and hat, brush them thoroughly with his old-fashioned, long handled clothes brush and add a bow tie to his clean shirt. Then he would go to Chapel morning and evening, just as he always had, ever since his boyhood in the 1880's when his job had been to pump the organ.

When my father came to manhood he acquired his own seat at the end of a pew. Here beneath the seat there was a slot for his Sunday hat. His Congregational Hymnary and the Bible his mother had given him in 1913 rested on the ledge in front of him. The books stayed on the ledge of his pew all the week while on Sundays now other, more energetic, hands pumped air into the organ.

Perhaps to be the child of my father's middle age brought me a security of its own, regardless of our changed circumstances, for he was set in his ways. This meant that many, many everyday things went on the same, just as they always had. *The Christian Herald*, for instance, arrived at the paper shop for us every week. This was an evangelical Christian newspaper founded in 1866 which my father had read all his life. It contained deeply Protestant news items and articles of general interest to devout chapel people, along with Bible stories and, above all, a children's page. There was always a rattling good serial on the children's page and I could not wait to read it.

When we had all read *The Christian Herald* my father, methodical as ever, would say gently to me, 'Put it away in the bottom drawer for the Union, my dear.' This was the form of words he always used, and I have no doubt the same words had been used by his father to him. What it meant was that the old copies were put in the bottom drawer of his old kneehole writing desk and when the drawer was full they were given to a local farmer who went regularly to the market at Sturminster Newton and who in turn would deliver them to the workhouse for the benefit of the inmates. Father's old Uncle George at Bagber had, my mother told me, been one of the Guardians of the workhouse all his life, so had his grandfather.

'What's a Guardian?' I wanted to know.

'Well, my mother explained.' 'It's someone who sees there is enough money and beds and food and things so that all the old people in the workhouse can be looked after properly.'

'But why do we say *The Christian Heralds* are for The Union?' I would persist.

My mother did not know. Mary didn't know either. I thought this was very poor. After all, Mary had left school now and was learning shorthand and typing with Miss Hobbs, whose brother kept the gents' outfitters in the High Street, so there was no excuse for her. Many, many years went by before I discovered that by the Poor Law Amendment Act of 1834 Unions of Parishes were formed to set up workhouses for the area they served, and the term 'Union' had been passed down by word of mouth ever since.

My father's other steadfast habit was reading *The News Chronicle* every day. That excellent old Liberal newspaper was readable, full of good sense and often very funny. It, too, had a children's page, with a feature called The Arkubs. These were Mr. and Mrs. Noah, their greedy and unsatisfactory son Japhet and all the animals in the Ark. They had glorious names. An ostrich was called Adelaide. A tortoise was called Oswald and my favourite of all was a little bear called Happy. In a quiet moment at school I would tell Miss Pope all about the Arkubs and she looked really interested.

In the evening, after tea, my father would get out his reading glasses, settle himself in his armchair and read bits of the News Chronicle to us. He read aloud in the monotonous, slightly wondering voice of a man not used to reading the printed word aloud and therefore rather impressed by it. Sometimes my mother, who was not always concentrating, would say,

'I can't follow that at all Arthur' and he would reply, having the last word:

'Well, that's what it says here.'

One of the useful consequences of our simple, hard-up life was that we made our own fun. Everybody did. Everybody was hard up too, so we all felt a sense of solidarity. We were unhindered by canned entertainment, except the glorious celluloid make-believe of the mobile cinema that came to the village every Monday evening, so our imagination ran free.

At the top of the stairs we had an old tin trunk. It was called the acting box and into it over the years had gone anything a child might delight to dress up in. There was, for instance, half of a beautiful Paisley shawl dating from about 1870. Heaven knows why there was only half, but my mother always maintained that old Aunt Em may have been a skilled cheesemaker but she had been eccentric enough for anything and had doubtless cut the Paisley shawl in half one dark night just to be trying. We never found the other half.

The acting box also contained a selection of striped calico underskirts that had belonged to Aunt Em. Long and full on her, they were gloriously trailing on me, and had to be held up in one hand before I could move. This had the effect of making me feel stately and elegant.

My great aunt had also had the forethought to leave behind a length of cream-coloured cheese cloth made from fine muslin and this was marvellous for more mundane roles. We had a book at school called *The Norman Maid* and a character in this, a faithful, devoted sort of girl, wore her hair in two braided golden plaits to her waist. My hair was fine and mousy and would not grow as far as my shoulders, but the thick, soft cheese cloth, braided with old dressing gown girdle, served me well. The minute this contraption was fairly on my head, I felt faithful and devoted and thoroughly Norman maidish and when Mary screamed with laughter I pretended not to notice.

The other high spot of the acting box was my mother's munition works' uniform. In the First World War my mother had been on the inspection staff of a munitions factory at Quedgeley in Gloucestershire. Part of the work had consisted of inspecting shells, the rest of inspecting the girls as they went into the works. They had to be strip searched in case they were taking matches into the munitions hall. It was a job she detested, for the girls were often not over keen on washing. My mother wore loose, straight, grey flannel trousers, a long and very ugly buttoned grey battle tunic and a matching pull on cap.

As a uniform it wouldn't have been out of place in a modern Chinese Commune, and in my childhood it could turn me into any male role you could think of, including the Prince Consort (with a bit of imagination) a soldier, a horse dealer and a railway guard. Or if I added Mary's lipstick and some gauzy scarves sneaked from her drawer when she was out, I was Lady Precious Stream.

We often acted in public in the village. I belonged to The King's Messengers, a missionary organisation which supported Church missions abroad, and sometimes The King's Messengers put on fund raising plays in the Junior School. In one of these I was a little black girl screaming in terror of evil spirits. I loved that.

Sometimes we had the chance to act at school during the day, in the presence of proud parents. In one of these plays, rehearsed thoroughly for weeks beforehand, Jennie got the part of a fairy, a real fairy with a wand, a frilly sticking-out white dress and wings, while I was a boy called Dick. At the end of the play, Jennie, wand in hand, had to say soulfully to me, as she prepared to go back to the fairy land she had come from: 'Goodbye, Dick, don't forget me.'

Now Jennie and I could always make each other laugh. We could send each other into fits as easily as most people breathe. Often we had no idea what it was that made us laugh so much. We simply felt that the same things were, or might be, funny. This meant that at the end of this play when Jennie said her farewell, I had to be careful to look straight past her. I couldn't risk looking at her.

We played a lot of party games. Church, chapel and school featured party games at their social evenings. We played musical chairs, statues, musical parcel, pin the tail on the donkey and Rigmarole Story. In this, one person begins a story then leaves off at a particularly exciting point and his neighbour takes it up. We also played 'My Aunt Fanny went to Paris', a hectic action game that involved imitating the goods – scissors, fan, bicycle, parrot and merry-go-round – with which Aunt Fanny staggered home through the Customs.

Games like these were often played at home at Christmas and birthday parties. The furniture was pushed back or taken out, Sandy the cat put out for the afternoon, and a noisy old wind-up gramophone, donated to my mother years before and intended for use outdoors, supplied the music. It had the authentic jazzy and foxtrotty tones of the period as it belted out 'Walking in a Winter Wonderland' or 'She Fell for a Fellow from Oopsala'.

Tea on such occasions was enormous, with jelly and blancmange, tinned fruit (a great treat), several sorts of jam with our bread and butter, and an iced cake with a suitable message on it, picked out with silver balls. Special occasion teas always seemed to be full of sweet things. Perhaps that is how we kept our energy up.

Anyway, the children's parties in my family had a riotous ending. Mary, who was by nature ingenious and dramatic, would organise tricks. In one of our favourites, each child was taken into the next room where two adults sat on chairs, with a horse blanket stretched right across the chairs and the space between, so that it looked as it they were sitting on a sofa. It was explained to the child that this was the King and Queen of Ruritania and she had been chosen to be Crown Princess, so she was to take her seat between Their Majesties for the Coronation. as she did so, their majesties stood up and the child fell through the horse blanket on to a pile of cushions on the floor. At this we all laughed uproariously, no matter how often we had seen it before.

For real sophistication in our village we had dancing. A group of five young men called the Five Swingers provided the music for socials in the Junior School, or else dances were held in The Hut. The dances were mostly waltzes and quicksteps, with an occasional foxtrot, well-liked but more difficult to do. We children made nuisances of ourselves, either dancing with each other, sliding about on the newly chalked floor, or badgering the grown ups to take us round the floor. The best bit for us was the Paul Jones. We all knew when the music required us to form a brisk circle and move round until the music stopped and we faced our partner for the next dance. The sight of one of us children caused many a partner's face to fall.

Dancing was the social highlight of our winters. In 1936 though there was no dancing at the traditional Church event after Christmas. King George V had died on 20th January and the Parish Social, held on 5th February, was considered too soon after the national bereavement. In fact, the Rector, who was said to have misgivings about the wisdom of allowing dancing at the end of Parish Socials anyway, even went so far as to consider cancelling the whole event. He must have realized how unpopular that would make him, so it was decided to go ahead with the social and simply cancel the dancing, ending with songs. That decision made him equally unpopular and it was said that the Five Swingers played at a dance elsewhere in the neighbourhood that very night. It was also said that some young people, never known to miss the parish social, went there and danced.

Mary belonged to the Girls' Association. This was an organisation for older teenage girls. They too put on entertainments, sophisticated affairs such as three-act plays, even thrillers, which was considered very daring. Or they put on concerts ending with groups of popular songs such as 'the Lily of Laguna' and for these they wore shimmering crepe or crepe paper dresses of glorious colours picked out skilfully by the local stage lighting experts.

In one of the plays she was in, Mary took the part of Lady Rhone Gelding, a horse-faced and hearty guest at a country house party deep in the English countryside. Mary approached the part with her usual zest. Someone lent her extremely well-cut jodhpurs and a tweed hacking jacket so that she really looked the part. The horsey image worried her though. She thought of herself as a tennis playing, fun loving member of the Girls' Association, who sang beautifully at their concerts. So she had a marcel wave for the play and her splendidly coiffed head softened the horsey look.

I decided to complain bitterly at this point that Mary's social life and activities were much ahead of mine, and it was all miserably and meanly unfair. The result of my complaints came swiftly, to my surprise. I was invited to go on a chapel outing to the Shillingstone hills. These hills were about eight miles away. That was not very far, of course, and the outline of the hills was clearly visible from the village, but still – it was the principle of the thing. It was a lovely outing. After games and a picnic tea, we children were all encouraged to roll down the hills – a glorious sensation. The slope was steep and one could roll quite fast. The Blackmore Vale lay spread out below and as I rolled, it seemed to be coming up the hill to meet me. It met me with all the scents of summer – bruised grass and crushed clover and moon daisies and a beautiful bee orchid, which, I'm ashamed to say, I picked. I put it in the pocket in my knickers and took it home to show my mother. It revived surprisingly well in a tooth-brush glass full of cold water from the pump room.

I really had no right to complain about my social life, or about any aspect of my life at all. There was a tremendous amount to do. The straightened funds of Dorset County Council's education budget were adequate enough to provide an educational school outing every summer term. Once we went to Windsor and saw the castle and then had a boat journey down the Thames.

Every summer term at school we had the school sports, mostly running races and balancing things, at which I was hopeless. And there was the Annual Flower Show. This was held in Stalbridge Park, beyond the churchyard, and we sat on grass humps and bumps, all that remained now of the rather splendid Jacobean house where Robert Boyle, the father of English chemistry, had lived and carried out some of his most famous experiments.

The Flower Show seemed to involve the entire village. Runner beans were measured and vegetable marrows anxiously watered for many an evening before it. Rabbits and poultry in cages lined the drive. There was a fancy dress parade for the children and any number of competitions, including skittling for a pig. A huge marquee contained the exhibits of needlework, knitting, fruit, vegetables, homemade cakes, honey and jam of every description. And for me the whole Flower Show was dominated by a rum-te-tum brass band and roundabouts. There were real fair ground roundabouts where the horses, painted in garish colours, had wide eyes and flaring nostrils.

Every bit as exciting though, to me, as any events organised by people outside, were the spontaneous summer family picnics we arranged ourselves. My mother would suddenly decide that if the fine weather held next day then we would have a picnic. A poultry farmer, Mr. Lukins, who owned a field beside Ten Acres, a dense, mysterious wood, was asked if we could light a fire on his ground, well away from the wood. He always agreed.

Next day about a dozen of us, with no effort as far as I could see, would arrive at the spot with teapot and mugs, a large water jug, baskets of food and an old black kettle kept for these occasions. One of the grown ups, usually Mary, took charge and dug out the fire base, Boy Scout fashion, while the rest of us scattered to the deep wood to find dry sticks. This took ages because by high summer the dead wood was all buried under foot high dogs' mercury and withered bluebell leaves.

It was a perfectly ordinary meal of sandwiches and cake, and the wood fire made the tea a bit smoky, but it all tasted marvellous for being out of doors. We played rounders and cricket until we grew too tired. Then we sang folk songs and rounds beside the dying embers until it was time to pack up the picnic remains and begin the long walk home.

Another summer Saturday was over. Soon the summer term would end and the long summer holidays begin. Before we broke up though, the most dreadful shock befell me. It was worse than anything it was possible to imagine, and nothing, nothing at all, had in any way prepared me for it. Miss Pope was leaving the Junior School. She was leaving to be married and she was going back to the Isle of Wight where she came from.

Even more dreadful, now the news was out, was that Miss Pope looked more beautiful than ever and everybody else seemed delighted. Everybody but me. A collection was made for a wedding present for her. There was a little ceremony in the class room one morning when the present was handed over, but all I could think of was the sinking feeling of purest misery in the pit of my stomach. Miss Pope was leaving. I was too miserable even to look at the present, to take in what it was. One good thing at least I could think of. Miss Pope was leaving the school but I should not have to return to the class room that had been hers. I was 'going up'. Next year I would be in Miss Pearse's class.

5

Miss Pearse

MISS PEARSE was extraordinary and much larger than life.
She was, I suppose, a fairly typical post First World War
spinster schoolteacher. Any hopes of matrimony she may ever
have had were doubtless extinguished by that war, which so
cruelly thinned the ranks of possible husbands. In any case,
women teachers in those days had to give up their careers upon
marriage, so would have thought long and hard before
marrying.

Miss Pearse was excitable, emotional and given to making a
fuss about trifles, such as a missing bottle of milk (hers) at
playtime. The milk was there, safely warming all the time
beside the tortoise stove. It had simply been obscured by a piece
of newspaper, but the fuss she made fairly rattled the whole
school.

She was a big woman with large hands and fingers and an
emotionally charged voice. There was always a vivid, intense
quality about her and she has left me with one of the most
extraordinary impressions of my childhood. She played the
violin and wore deeply cut jersey suits, made decent in front by
the beige tussore modesty vests of the times. She played music
of a flamboyant and emotional nature on her violin, which was
matched by her manner of playing. An ecstatic smile might
sometimes spread across her face and she might nod or sway in
time to the music, or she might look away into the distance as
if transfixed by what she saw there. During Miss Pearse's often
public performances on the violin everyone was, of course, very
quiet. Nobody spoke or dared to move. I watched her closely

and I shall treasure for ever the general impression I have in my head of those events, an impression of a large, heaving jersey clad bosom, a dancing tussore modesty vest and a somewhat screechy violin all a little out of phase with each other.

Miss Pearse's command of voice and gesture was amazing and I found myself watching and listening closely to her out of sheer interest at seeing what could possibly come next. Her bright greenish eyes seemed to be everywhere at once (and she never missed anything). Her large hands and fingers were never still and her voice, tremulous, modulated, lyrical, admonishing, scolding or occasionally bawling, was never quiet. Never, that is, except when she had commanded absolute concentration and quiet and the class was writing. Then she would also be quiet, but at these times, when I stole a look at her, I wondered if she might burst.

Miss Pearse had a certain tendency to 'go on' about things, things which irritated her, or put her about. My mother shared the same characteristics, though in a more collected fashion. When she did so, my father would listen patiently and when, as inevitably happened, my mother had to pause and draw breath, my father would say gently 'True, oh Queen.' This had the effect of stopping my mother in full flow, it was so unexpected, and made us all roar with laughter. It also had the useful effect of allowing my father to get on undisturbed with whatever he had been doing before the outburst from my mother interrupted him.

What, I used to wonder, would have happened if Miss Pearse had 'gone on' about something in my father's hearing. Suddenly, one day as Miss Pearse was holding forth with some irritation, and I was sitting at the double desk I shared with Ivor Davidson, both of us looking a little anxiously at the brass inkwell covers, I felt I had the answer. Father would simply have gone where he could not hear her, quite early in the tirade, and there would have been no laughter.

All the same, I respected Miss Pearse's methods. She made us

work hard. We had for instance to write out sentences
explaining the difference between 'hear with your ears' and
'put it down here' while the register was being marked.

'You see Mr. Duncan,' she explained to the school attendance
officer who called in the middle of this and looked impressed.
'We are so busy we simply have to work while the register is
being marked. We must use our time productively.'

This was not just a gambit to impress, it happened regularly
and gave the class a series of useful lessons learned early.

Above all, her own emotional nature endowed her with a gift
for story telling. I can well recall waking up with an exalted
feeling deep inside me on Monday and Tuesday mornings and
thinking to myself 'It's Old Testament stories today.' I would
hurry to school and after prayers and a hymn and register Miss
Pearse would gather us around her in a big semi-circle and
begin. The details of the story of the child Samuel called, as he
thought, by Eli, but in fact by the Lord, particularly gripped
me. I felt I was there. I felt the stillness of the Old Testament
night, the chill of fear as Samuel awoke. I heard his bare
pattering feet on linoleum, just like the lino on our upstairs
landing at home, as he went to the old man. If this was religious
instruction, then I loved it. And her description of the crossing
of the Red Sea by the Israelites made the hairs on the back of
my neck stand up.

The Red Sea, she explained, divided and gave the Israelites a
path of dry land through the sea, with a wall on either side of
them, like going through a ripe corn field only higher, until they
were all safely on the other side.

'Then all Pharaoh's horses and chariots came thundering
after them on to the dry path. The horsemen went first, then
one of them in front suddenly said "this ground is a bit sloppy."
Then another one leaned over in his saddle and said "It's
getting really sloppy and the horses' hooves are splashing."'

And so on, with Miss Pearse's wonderful sense of theatre
building the scene up to a climax where all the Egyptians were

drowned and the sea washed over them, so that you could not see where the path had been.

Religious instruction at the Junior School followed a set pattern. We had Old Testament on Mondays and Tuesdays, New Testament on Wednesdays, Prayer Book on Thursdays and hymns, lovely, tuneful hymns on Fridays. Some of them were chosen by Miss Pearse as appropriate to the season or the festival, but some the class could choose. One Friday Ivor Davidson, sitting next to me, chose 'Immortal, Invisible, God Only Wise'.

'No,' said Miss Pearse firmly. 'You can't have that. You don't know what it means.' Such was her enthusiasm for learning that we found out by ourselves exactly what it meant and next week confronted her with our knowledge. She relented at once, and afterwards we chose that hymn most Fridays.

Miss Pearse's immense energy had, mercifully, many channels and she was by nature and training extremely thorough. Any subject on earth which she gave her mind to immediately benefitted from being listed and categorised in her excellent clear script and greatly expanded by continual research. It then became a matter for considerable critical study and loquacious commentary. Nature study gave her just the scope she needed for her enthusiasm and natural gifts. Nature study was part of the curriculum and we had a nature table in one corner of the classroom. All the children were encouraged to bring the first flowers, and sometimes weeds, of the season to school for the nature table. They were put in water in glass fish paste jars neatly labelled in Miss Pearse's beautiful script. Every year the small prize for the most firsts was won by a girl called May Blake who lived in a sheltered hollow by the brook at Poolstown a mile away.

I envied May Blake with all my heart. Hours spent searching the bluebell woods of Harpitts and Ten Acre, the cowslip banks beside the single track of the railway line within sight of Hewletts Farm, or the reedy cuckoo flower fields at Prior's

Down, never produced any first for me. Each flower on the nature table had a glass fish paste jar to itself, so we could clearly see the formation of leaves, stem, stamens and seed sacs, about all of which Miss Pearse was amazingly well-informed.

We, my family, were now well settled in the old house, a large allotment had been acquired and the garden belonging to the house disciplined. This was a little walled garden beside the old stables adjoining the house, which for centuries must have been an ashpit and general rubbish dump. The soil was incredibly poor for such an area and Mary and I, digging enthusiastically for buried treasure, found endless pieces of crockery and china. Some of the pieces were a pretty shade of blue, but we never managed to fit them together to make anything. One day, with great excitement, we dug up a clay pipe with a pretty design round the bowl, but we soon found it had no stem, which was probably why it had been consigned to the ash heap in the first place.

'Why can't we grow things here like everywhere else?' Mary asked one day, slashing back some ivy.

'They do say,' my father remarked after some thought, 'that the common buddleia will grow in anything.'

That was enough for Mary. She searched the village until she had located a common buddleia which was, in fact, not common at all in those parts, and begged a cutting. She then put it in the very centre of the barren, gritty little plot and we went in to tea.

Whatever was in that plot suited the buddleia. It took root and grew and grew, hanging with mauve blossoms and attracting wave upon wave of immigrant butterflies. Sandy the cat could climb its woody stem and disappear. Pruning, which it got every few months, only seemed to provoke it to bigger, longer, mauver blossoms, and people in the village remarked that they had never seen anything like it. I thought perhaps Miss Pearse had never seen anything like it either, so I tried to tell her about our remarkable buddleia in the old rubbish dump. She did not listen. The faculty of listening, of being really interested in what one was saying that Miss Pope had possessed to such a degree, was one that Miss Pearse did not possess at all. So I tried another tack.

'Can we have some on the nature table?' I asked.

'No' Miss Pearse replied firmly. 'The nature table is for wild flowers.' So I never did get anything on the nature table, neatly labelled and with my name on it.

All the same, I loved the subject of nature study, and it was made ever more interesting for us by nature walks. Leaves, flowers, trees, bark, the shape of different birds' nests, their positions and height in the trees, the shape of clouds, the forecasting of weather, the names and habits of all the grasses and weeds beneath our feet and the ancestry of the earth and stones in the gateways of every field we entered – all these Miss Pearse knew about. Incredibly observant herself, she taught us to use our eyes.

We also had a series of lessons, probably inspired by the County Council, about different aspects of health and hygiene, followed where possible, given our limited cloakroom facilities, by a practical session. Miss Pearse, with her gift for dramatic narration, would describe to us the environment, life style, habits and, given the chance, success, of the average germ. Pictures were shown to us of the structure of gums and teeth, and we were told the correct way to clean our teeth, to brush up and down, not backwards and forwards

When the time came for a practical session, she placed a large bowl on the table in the front of the class, produced junior sized toothbrushes and a dollop of pink toothpaste for each child and commanded us to clean our teeth properly and thoroughly, then spit into the bowl. We entered into all this with incredible thoroughness, especially the spitting, the boys being able, apparently by nature, to spit with extreme accuracy and reach more distant targets.

'Cleanliness,' my mother would remark, catching my father's

eye for just an instant when I told her about the health lessons, 'Is next to Godliness.' And when I told her about the spitting and how good the boys were at it, she added, 'And no doubt the good Lord gave them their skill at spitting too.'

There were, my mother would have agreed with Miss Pearse, had her opinion been sought and actually listened to, two sorts of people. Those who were clean and those who were not. Neither allowed of borderline cases. In our house all washing that could be boiled was boiled, even though it meant my mother getting up early to light the fire beneath the copper, and everything, boiled or not, was washed by hand, over all its surface, with big bars of green soap called Puritan. This, in addition to the use of proprietary brands of soap powder like Rinso and Oxydol, for which my mother thought the makers made extravagant claims. Washing up was done in water to which a liberal pinch of washing soda and a large handful of soapflakes had been added, the soda to cope with grease and the soap to do the rest of the cleaning.

To wash ourselves we had a well-known brand of absolutely white soap called Knights Castile. 'We do not' my mother would say firmly 'want anything too highly scented. We don't want the whole neighbourhood to know when we are having a wash.'

That to my mother's mind would be overdoing it, showing off, attitudes she detested. However, cleanliness being with us such a strong point with us, I was in a good position when Miss Pearse decided, shortly after the tooth care demonstration, that to do games and gym in dresses was unhealthy and restrictive. There were no special garments for our sessions of physical jerks in the yard, to which we filed out in pairs of girls. There was not a great deal by way of equipment, just a ball or two, bean bags and stumps, bat and ball for rounders, so our physical exercise was what we made it. And now, this bright sunny morning, Miss Pearse was suggesting that our cotton frocks were unsuitable for gym and it would be much more healthy if we took them off and appeared in our underwear. We considered this. Some members of the class were clearly appalled. Then I remembered that under my faded, puff-sleeved, passed-down-from-Betty-Lang cotton frock I had a cotton vest as white as snow and pale blue knickers clean on that day. It had all looked rather nice when I dressed that morning. I stripped my dress off and pranced about the class room all skinny eight-year-old arms and legs, enjoying the unexpected opportunity quite hugely.

A few other little girls followed my example and took their dresses off but the rest looked stony faced and prim and filed out into the yard fully clothed. Physical jerks in one's underwear in the yard was a lovely sensation. I had no idea it could be so enjoyable.

That evening my mother remarked, to my astonishment. 'I saw you prancing round the yard in your vest and knickers as I went past the end of the lane today, so I went down and looked through the railings. Several other little girls had taken their dresses off. I wanted to make sure it was not just you. Why were you doing that?'

'Miss Pearse says it's much healthier,' I said quickly. 'You get freedom of movement and the air gets to you. We're doing health care now, teeth and things. I told you.'

'Oh I see,' said my mother, unconvinced.

I realised that my mother thought most schoolteachers odd and Miss Pearse odder than most. On the whole she approved of the headmistress's methods and felt she was an extremely good teacher, if an alarmingly excitable woman. I could simply not have faced any confrontation between those two. My mother would, I had no doubt, have won, but the loquacity we should all have had to endure before Miss Pearse conceded defeat made my blood run cold and my knees feel quite weak. That was why I felt it wiser not to tell my mother abut the Scott child.

A little girl named Scott had been killed in the High Street by a coal lorry a few years before. She had of course been a pupil at the school and Miss Pearse had been fond of her.

'She is never far away from us.' She would tell us, her eyes glittering as she nodded gravely. 'I know she is with us in spirit. Sometimes I feel her little hand in mine, here in this room. Sometimes I hear her voice quite clearly here in this very classroom.'

We worked hard. With Miss Pearse in charge no-one would have dared to slack, but our school days were not all lessons. We sang. Oh, how we sang. Not just hymns but singing lessons around the school piano and simple folk songs were very popular.

'Johnny Come Down from Hilo', 'The Girl I Left Behind Me' and 'Speed Bonnie Boat' were all sung with gusto. We knew that if we sang heartily we would be able to tackle much more complicated songs when we went to the Top School, the Senior School on Church Hill, at the age of nine. Snatches of these songs floated down to us – the Twenty Third Psalm set to Brother James's Air, a song called 'Strawberry Fair' with a chorus that went 'Rifol, Rifol, Stick in a Trifle (or so we thought) and the lovely Welsh song 'The Ash Grove'. We in the Junior School all looked forward to that.

We danced a lot. Boys as well as girls danced simple English Country Dances to tunes called 'Rufty Tufty', 'Selinger's Round', 'Brighton Camp' and 'Gathering Peascods' and we marked the seasons of the year with our singing. Hymns were chosen for whatever aspect of the Church's calendar we had reached and Miss Pearse was an expert in knowing just where we were in that. But we marked other seasons too with songs or stories. Oak Apple Day was always kept. Miss Pearse would bring oak leaves and oak apples to school and explain how Charles II had hidden in a huge English oak tree. She explained in vivid detail the shivering, sweating fear he felt as Cromwell's soldiers, with heads like pudding basins, searched for him underneath. And when they gave up and went away, oh then,

Charles mopped his brow with the back of his hand and smiled a broad smile of relief as he stretched his long legs nervously, making quite sure that no branches cracked as he did so. It was marvellous, I always thought, how Miss Pearse knew all this.

Another event we celebrated with tremendous fervour was Empire Day on 24th May. That week we had lessons about the Empire and the creation of the Dominions.

'Then after a long time of being in the Empire, the King and the Prime Minister said to the governments of Canada and Australia "Well, do you think you'd like to rule yourselves now?"' Miss Pearse said, reducing the whole complex matter to one of absolute simplicity, easily understood by an eight-year-old.

Pictures of various parts of the Empire, particularly pictures with children in them, were put up round the walls, and a flag appeared, which we did not usually have in the classroom. For several weeks we had rehearsed a little programme of suitable and largely patriotic songs. Then, on the day, we stood on our chairs to sing them in front of parents, well mothers anyway, fathers were at work, invited in for the occasion. The classroom was especially tidied up and more flowers put out. Bunches of flowers, red, white and blue, if possible, for Empire Day were put on the tables. We were now out of the glass fish paste jar league and into old stone-coloured Keiller marmalade jars.

I spent two years in Miss Pearse's class. We gave a lot of time to learning to write clearly and well. For our joined up writing we used wooden-handled dipper pens. These had very sturdy metal nibs, which could be changed when worn out, a messy job sometimes requiring a lot of strength. We dipped our pens in the inkwells found in the right hand corner of each desk and scratched away, holding our pens along the line of our first fingers, to give it control and look professional. We often had to learn things by heart, spelling, grammar and above all, the multiplication tables up to the twelve-times tables. We were drilled with them until we could reproduce the word perfect monotonous sing-song beloved of films of 1930's schools.

We did a lot of sums, which I found hard, and composition which I found easy. We read aloud and recited poetry and acted in plays, for parents, or for raising money for Church causes, notably missions, and of course, the day always started with a hymn, prayers and scripture or religious observance in some form. These often took the form of a story or explanation from Miss Pearse, followed by a question and answer session. Her true actor's feel for her audience, her innate sense of theatre never deserted her. Her bright eyes seemed to be everywhere, her mobile face and waving hands were never still and we tumbled over ourselves to provide answers. It was all the purest, most effective theatre. No child ever felt left out and no child could possibly have been bored, we were all too anxious to see what was coming next.

One morning, a Thursday and so Prayer Book morning, Miss Pearse called six of us, three boys and three girls, out of the class and set the catechism before us.

'Learn it,' she said firmly 'And when you know it off by heart I will ask you questions about it and see if you have understood it.'

We set to work, having no idea why. A few Thursdays later we could parrot it off. I can to this day recite huge chunks about keeping my hands from picking and stealing, my tongue from evil speaking, lying and slandering. And ever more resonantly.

'I renounce the Devil and all his works, the pomps and vanities of this wicked work and all the sinful lusts of the flesh.'

I love the sound of the words, as I loved them then, and our little group was carried along on the rhythm of them.

Miss Pearse came to test our comprehension. 'Ask me about the catechism.' She said, smiling. We did. We bombarded her with questions.

'What was adultery?' we asked. 'What was fornication?' I wanted to know, in a shrill voice, exactly what was meant by all the sinful lusts of the flesh. She did her best to explain, but she was a maiden lady, it was a Church school and were, after all, not yet nine years old. We were profoundly dissatisfied. All her explanations of everything, we pointed out accusingly, might perfectly well apply to picking and stealing, so if it was all the same thing why did we have to learn about sinful lusts and adultery.

The results of this conversation became clear the following week. We had all been selected to be coached for the scholarship and would be put in for it a year early – next year at the Top School on Church Hill. We would be just ten years old by then, or in my case not quite, and if we failed the Scholarship at the first attempt it did not matter, we would be put in for it again the next year as if nothing had happened.

It was a random and unorthodox method of selection, Miss Pearse taking the view that if we were ready to deliberate abstract ideas, such as the sinful lusts of the flesh, then we were quite ready for the extra compositions and coaching in sums that would be the prelude to taking the scholarship a year early. In fact, the coaching took the form of being given special work and getting on with it in our own little group. We could discuss ideas with each other if we wished, but not sums, or we might have copied. There was a lot of merit in this method. We could get on at a good speed, which Miss Pearse's own tremendous enthusiasm for learning inspired us to do and to regard as absolutely normal. There was also merit in it for her, too, as she could then devote more time to the slower ones in the class.

A great deal of our reading matter was, I am glad to say, simpler than the catechism. Miss Pearse read aloud books like *Winnie the Pooh* and *The Wind in the Willows*. Such books were perfect vehicles for her and the class was absolutely fascinated. She was slow-witted, deep voiced Pooh, squeaky Piglet, fussy Kanga and babyish Roo, all within minutes, while her Ratty and Mole had me clasping my fingers tightly together and wishing the lesson would never end.

In addition to these books I was often lent others by people in the village. My eyes always strayed towards their bookshelves as soon as I was fairly inside someone's house, so I suppose the point that I was a bookworm was made early. Sometimes, however, the books offered to me were not considered suitable by my mother. Her own tastes were wide and she was extremely broad minded, but she knew her own child, so 'Uncle Tom's Cabin' had to be sent back unopened, with a note of thanks and the excuse that I was too young for it. Later, though, I overheard her saying to my father

'That child is all too ready to have nightmares as it is, Arthur, without bringing material into this house to set off some more.'

Sometimes, of course, books were bought for the school, for the sheer pleasure of reading and not as textbooks. The County Council's Education Committee had a small budget for the purpose and I have no doubt whatever that Miss Pearse had a say in how our share of it was spent. The cinema, she well knew, was of tremendous interest for all of us and our families and we, her class, were much of an age with Shirley Temple. Jane Withers was older than us and Mickey Rooney and Freddie Bartholomew may have been glamorous child stars but they were boys. Shirley Temple was different. She laughed and danced and sang and didn't fuss with her clothes. Success had not spoiled her, even though by 1937 she had been a box office star for three years.

It could, we felt, have happened to us and the fact that it hadn't did not make us in the least bit envious of Shirley Temple. True, she did have a lot of pretty clothes, and she didn't seem to have to go to school all that regularly, but she had to spend an awful lot of time with grown ups.

So, when Miss Pearse ordered books there were sure to be some about the cinema, and one day a lovely, shining book about Shirley Temple was unpacked out of the crate from County Hall delivered to the school. It was a fat book smelling of printer's ink and full of interesting pictures about the young

film star's life. I couldn't wait to read this book. I wanted to see
if Shirley Temple got anything wrong. Perhaps, because I could
read quickly, Miss Pearse would let me borrow it first. The
class went very quiet. We waited expectantly, then Miss Pearse
said firmly, 'I want Eldred to have this book first.' Eldred
smiled delightedly as Miss Pearse took it to his desk.

Eldred had a calliper on his leg and could only walk slowly.
But he *read* slowly too. Surely Miss Pearse knew that, I thought
bitterly, as I walked home along the High Street after home
going prayers at 4 o'clock, on which I could not concentrate at
all. Really, she was extraordinary. Yes, my mother was right
again. Miss Pearse was odd. I kicked a stone along the gutter
as far as the old house and went indoors, scowling.

6

The Seasons of the Year

THE SEASONS in this secluded vale were the framework of our lives. The Church's year reached back to the fertility rites and pagan symbols of Easter eggs and mistletoe and much of what happened then and now was governed by the weather. The weather determined farming – and farming in all its forms was the backbone of village life. Estate cottages, first Anglesey Cottages, later Westminster Cottages built in the nineteenth century around The Ring, always had large gardens. In the Anglesey group they had pigsties so that the estate workers could be as self-sufficient as possible.

The Ring, triangular in shape, is a nicely shaped piece of grass steeply banked towards the Lower Road, with rose beds and, after the Coronation of George VI in 1937, a handsome wooden seat with, inscribed on a plate fixed to the back the words, 'Rest and Be Thankful'. It was a large, sturdy seat and the square, red-tiled surface on which it was mounted kept one's feet dry.

An old lady who had worked hard all her life came out of a house nearby to inspect the seat. When she read the inscription she retorted sharply,

'I ain't got no time to rest and be thankful,' and went home.

The Ring had in earlier times been a bull ring and the name stuck. The Westminster Cottages and farms had the Westminster arms of a wheatsheaf engraved on them: it also appeared again in a particularly striking and rather nasty shade of yellow on the formal hats and caps of the village schools.

Just beyond The Ring was the blacksmith's forge. The family, named Jeans, had been blacksmiths on that spot from father to son since the Middle Ages. Here farming supported them throughout the year. Chain harrows, hay rakes, mowing machines and every sort of cart could be seen there undergoing repairs. Throughout the year horses were brought in to be shod. The forge had small leaded window panes and a stable door. I was just tall enough to see over the bolted bottom half to where shaky flames threw long shadows up the wall, sparks struck off the anvil and the horse scraped his hooves on the old flagged floor. The blacksmith wore a leather apron and held the hoof being shod against it, talking gently to the nervous animal through the cloud of smoke that rose into his face from the hoof.

The seasons in those days seemed more straightforward so that we seemed to know exactly where we were with the weather. The autumn was Keats's season of mists, and for part of the autumn it rained. There may have been spells of dry sunny weather such as a St. Luke's Summer (around St. Luke's Day on the 18th of October), but by, or shortly after, All Saints Day (1st November) the rain usually set in in earnest. The heavy Oxford clay that the village was built on retaliated with a sea of mud.

'There's two sorts of rain,' my father would say. 'Town rain where people don't really get wet at all, and country rain where not even a sack bag will keep it out on a bad day.'

The sack bag was an unused meal sack, brightish yellow and tightly woven from jute, which my father would fasten round his shoulders like a cape over his raincoat. It was effective in keeping the rain off him because it was so slowly absorbent itself, but when he took it off it was so sodden with rain I couldn't lift it. All this rain on our clay soil produced mud that had to be seen to be believed. The gateway of every field was stogged in mud. There was then a real risk that children's wellingtons would sink into it so firmly that a foot with a sock on it would come out of the boot, leaving the wellington still in place. The child caught like this tried hard to balance on one leg and regain the mudbound boot, but more often foot, sock and knee got very muddy. 'I got stuck in the mud,' was a condition of dishevelment readily understood by my mother.

Ditches and drains had to be kept clear all the year so that they were fit to cope with the gallons of water that came through them in the autumn and winter. Clay ground like this, though, meant good, rich dairy pasture and cows did well in the Blackmore Vale. Cows, I noticed, had their own method of dealing with the mud. As they filed home daily across the home ground they made permanent deep ruts in the ground, packing the earth down so hard with their hooves over centuries, that the rain didn't seem to penetrate these dips. The ruts perfectly fitted their hoof fall as they walked, so they got over the ground and into the cowstall surprisingly quickly.

On 5th November we always kept Guy Fawkes night at home. I think many people did in those days. We had a small bonfire in the little walled garden, the former ashpit where the buddleia grew. The soil was so ashy already that a bit more ash didn't matter, and we had a guy made out of straw and sacking. We had fireworks, we saved up for them for weeks, but my father did not care for loud bangs, so he stayed indoors. Mary officiated with her usual enthusiasm, pinning Catherine wheels in place expertly and letting off the one big rocket which we always saved to the end. I ran about in the darkness with sparklers, shrieking with excitement.

The frosts came eventually making the muddy ground much easier to get around on. Everyone hoped for frost by Christmas. Mild and muggy weather was felt to be unhealthy and dangerous for the village.

'A green Christmas and a full Churchyard,' people would remark gravely to my mother as we passed them in the High Street. I felt irritated by this pessimism. What an attitude! Christmas was, after all, Christmas no matter what the weather was like, with presents arriving every day and being hidden.

Christmas Day had a set pattern – at least it had for me. It began with stocking opening, mostly oranges, nuts, a penny or two carefully wrapped, and perhaps a small bakelite toy. Then downstairs for breakfast – porridge and bacon and eggs and a second helping of porridge for Sandy the cat. Hard up we may have been but simple presents done up with brown paper and string, sent to us by relations and arriving via the postman's bicycle, created enormous excitement. We opened them all together around the dining room table, which we had to clear hastily when dinner was ready. Christmas dinner was always a big stuffed chicken with roast potatoes and our own sprouts and cabbage. We had no vegetable garden where we lived now but my father had been able rent a large allotment nearby, reached through a covered alleyway between some cottages, where all manner of vegetables grew well.

My parents did not care for goose, and duck, though available, was said to be a mean bird with no breast on it. Turkey we did not seem to have heard of, and I cannot remember that anyone had it in the village. The chicken was of course followed by my mother's Christmas pudding, made weeks before with real candied peel, halves of lemon and oranges with rock hard candy sugar set inside them. I always offered to help slice these. We ate the pudding, made to my mother's traditional recipe and very dark, with custard, never cream.

Tea on Christmas Day was usually bread and butter, Christmas present biscuits if any had been given us, and the traditional Christmas cake made by my mother and decorated by Mary with silver balls, hard as ball bearings when you bit them, though they tasted quite good, saying 'A Happy Christmas.'

Boxing Day was quite different from Christmas Day. It was cold meat and bubble and squeak for lunch and if possible lots of fresh air all day. On Boxing Day morning we went to see the meet. The local pack of fox hounds had as its Master of Fox

Hounds a woman, Miss Guest, whose mother, before she became Lady Theodora Guest of Innwood near Henstridge, had been Lady Theodora Grosvenor, sister of the first Duke of Westminster.

Miss Guest looked a bit formidable, with a grim manner and peremptory voice and the people who worked for her always seemed in awe of her. She always rode side saddle, with a long, dark riding habit falling gracefully across her saddle. I felt, from reading books like 'The Oak Staircase' and various children's historical books, that women who rode side saddle in elegant riding habits must possess an image of romantic femininity. Miss Guest did not. She sat bolt upright, shouting instructions so fiercely that the people who began by being in awe of her ended up apparently terrified.

We saw the hounds assemble at a local inn and watched fascinated while the stirrup cup was offered to the huntsmen and, at a signal from the Master of Foxhounds, the hunt moved off. Many village people followed the hounds on foot or by bicycle but Mary and I, who had probably had a long walk to get to the meet, generally went home.

Soon after we moved to the village Auntie Millie and the husband she had lived with in Bristol parted, and she went to London, becoming a buyer in the fabrics department of a famous Oxford Street store. One consequence of this was that she found all sorts of little novelties and extras in the London of those days and sent or brought them to us. Another consequence was that now she had no home of her own she always came to spend Christmas with us. Excitement at the prospect mounted all day. Mary and I always met her train and the Christmas Eve trains were often unusually late. This meant either that we would go home again and return to the station at intervals, or wait patiently. I would sit in the waiting room beside Mary on a hard wooden bench against the wall, with my feet not touching the scrubbed bare floor. The station staff kept good fires and Stalbridge station building was brick-built and stout, so we were warm enough. Warm enough that is, except for a few howling draughts whenever people came in to speak through a wooden hatch to the clerk in the ticket office, or to buy tickets.

Quite a crowd of village people would gather in the waiting room as the train, bearing various relations, was expected, and finally word went round among the watchers 'She's off of Templecombe' or 'Ee's left Henstridge'. The sturdy white crossing gates would open and bang back into a locked position. If it was dark a red lamp would glow in the middle of each gate to warn the carts, vans and bicycles that might still be on the road, and we would hurry across the line over some sleepers in front of the signal box to 'the other side'. The expression 'going across to the other side' on the station always made me think of hymns about going to Heaven.

In fact, we went to a little stone-built shelter, big enough to seat about a dozen people, again on hard benches on three sides and a window at each end so that we could look up and down the track. A large part of the front of this shelter was open and looked on to the line. The roof extended in a peak out over the platform, making an efficient shelter from the worst of the wind and driving rain.

Finally, the Henstridge signal went down, the little local train puffed self-importantly down the slope to a stop, dead level with the platform, and Auntie Millie got out, to be smothered with our exuberant hugs and kisses. She was easily the best dressed of all the passengers who got down at Stalbridge Station on a Christmas Eve, we felt. Dark and vivacious, heads turned to look at her and her vitality always seemed to me to make everybody else look half dead. All the same, we always offered to help her carry her various interesting looking parcels.

We rarely had snow in winter, and I was frankly glad of it, for the horrid boys would have pelted us with snowballs, persistently and with quite deadly accuracy, making our lives a misery whenever we went out. I loved the January frosts and the slowly lengthening evenings. Then, early in February, searching hard among the dark green leaves of the steep banks at the top of the hill at Bazel Bridge, my father and I would find the first white violets of spring. We were always delighted when we found some, often not more than three or four. We carried them home proudly, telling each other how lovely they smelt, and how pleased my mother would be.

Spring in Stalbridge was marked out in its progress for us by, first of all, the rolling names given by the Church to the various Sundays before Lent. We'd had Epiphany of course, starting just after Christmas but now, as Lent approached, we had the gloriously named Septuagesima, Sexagesima and Quinquagesima. I always loved the sound of those names, even when I had no idea what they meant. Then as the Sundays of the Church's year rolled on, so we had bigger and more colourful flowers than those first white violets. I always felt there was a connection there.

Primroses grew everywhere, on mossy banks above streams, in woods and copses and in most of the undisturbed hedges of the fields. Primroses always seemed to me to be the flowers of Lent and it was generally not until after Easter that we found cowslips and bluebells. Later still, getting towards Ascension Day or even Whitsun, we found Ragged Robins, or red campion, in all the hedges, and cuckoo flowers among the reeds of the – generally rather badly drained – fields below the village.

In the spring we hatched little chickens. We kept hens whenever we had room. Many country people did if they had a large garden or orchard. The hens were generally Light Sussex, white with a necklace of black feathers, or the magnificent Rhode Island Reds. Rhode Islands were a lovely reddish brown colour with thick horny legs and strong well-made feet. The hens were paler, neat and trim especially viewed from behind. The cock birds were dark red, proud looking and, to my childish eyes, perpetually bad tempered.

When they went broody the hens sat on a clutch of twelve eggs for three weeks. At the end of that time, given good luck and no foxes breaking in, a dozen lovely little chicks appeared, only to scuttle back under Mum if we tried to get too close.

If for any reason the chicks could not stay with the hen they were put in a hoover. Yes, what we knew as a hoover was a little pen with a lamp in the middle for warmth. The placing of this lamp was important as the heat drew the chickens together in the middle of the pen, and stopped them from crowding into corners and suffocating each other.

Our hens were in a big run almost the length of the garden, from which they eyed us beadily through the wire netting, only getting excited if we were seen to be carrying an old cocoa tin. Into the cocoa tin went earth worms while we were digging, and when we had enough we would lob them over the wirenetting. Then the normally sedate old biddies squawked and flapped and got wildly excited.

The hens kept by many people in the village were almost completely free range, though barricaded out of gardens of course. The hens from Home Farm near the school wandered down the lane all day pecking and foraging, unless an occasional baker's van or Austin Seven came by. Then they would dash for home as fast as their horny Rhode Island legs could carry them, squawking with terror. It was all so different from their normal self-important 'pawk, pawk, pawk, pawk' when things were going well, or their self congratulating, cheerful 'Puck, puck, puck, puck, puck egg' when they had just laid an egg.

As well as foraging, the hens were fed well. They got maize and meal and every scrap of kitchen waste. Potato peelings were carefully boiled in a pan on a smelly old primus stove until soft and added to the meal. It was a task and a smell that gave my mother a lifelong loathing of potatoes served in their skins at the table. Generally the hens were fed from heavy, clanking metal buckets which were filled up in the mealhouse with scoops made from wood or aluminium. Very occasionally a traditional yoke was used to carry the buckets. A yoke was a smooth, shaped piece of wood which fitted surprisingly comfortably across the shoulders, with chains at each side ending in hooks from which buckets were hung. The word 'Yoke' is an Old Norse word, so I suppose the practice had been around for a long time.

In the spring the cows were out all the time. They were called in for milking with a traditional cow call I have only heard in the Blackmore Vale. It sounded something like 'How up, How up, How a, How a, How a' and it was extremely effective. At milking time the Vale echoed with the sound of many herds being called. The human voice could send it out on a warm afternoon over forty acres of ground, or so it seemed when cows almost out of sight straightaway lumbered heavily to their feet.

When the cows reached the cowstalls, they were tethered with a loose chain, each cow knowing her place and milked by hand. The milkers sat on three-legged stools and one of my earliest memories is of an old cowman who would settle himself on his milking stool, turn back the brim of his battered hat, lean his hat companionably against the cow's flank and sing 'Abide with me'. Over and over he sang in a monotonous, rather tuneless voice, because, he said, 'It did make 'er give 'er milk down a treat.'

Summer brought our rich dairy ground into lush mowing grass with moon daisies and clover in it. I always sensed that our mowing grass was guarded. It was securely fenced of course to keep cattle out and no human foot ever trod through it.

'A ton of June hay is worth two tons of August hay' my father would say and when I asked why he replied simply, 'There's so much more goodness in it.'

I watched the mowing grass anxiously I saw how the wind tore through it, turning it silvery and green with light and shade, noticed it growing taller and somehow thicker. It was like looking at the promised land. Then suddenly one fine June morning at Thornhill, there was old Tom the cob. He was <u>in</u> the mowing grass, right out across the ground with the mowing machine, the precious mowing grass falling in swathes. I felt a profound sense of shock whenever I saw mowing grass being cut.

The hay was turned, then the dry hay was carried, usually in the big waggon drawn by Chink to the rick yard. It had to be absolutely dry of course or you got a hot rick, possibly a fire. This was bad enough in itself for it meant a big loss, but it also earned the farmer who had this misfortune the scorn of other farmers who felt he had simply made a bad error of judgement.

I loved to watch the rick being made, the base set up carefully first, then the edges of the rick firmly and continually filled out and trodden down as it grew. To a small child it was a wonder to look at, though the men who had all the labour of it didn't see it like that. My mother's contribution to this busy time was to send flasks of tea and slabs of her farmhouse cake down to the hay fields. The cake, always the same, was a very moist and filling fruit cake and we loved it.

An unusual, rather private, excitement came to me and my friends around midsummer – a roadworking team came to the village. Tar, smelly hot tar, was spread all over the road by a machine, then labourers in the tarry vineyard threw fine gravel and grit all over the tar. After that, a huge steam roller huffed and puffed and rolled it back and forth, half the road (lengthways) at a time, until all the fine stones were pressed into the tar, leaving a firm, smooth surface.

The team moved on and it was then that we little girls really began to enjoy ourselves. The warm tar had been pressed down by the steamroller so that it ran in rivulets to the sides of the road. If the day was really hot the tar formed into fat, black bubbles. That was when my friends and I came into our own. We wore daps – light, black, fabric gym shoes with rubberised soles – and when our daps-clad foot was brought down on the tar bubbles they popped with a most satisfying pop.

Later in the summer while the schools were still on holiday we had the annual Flower Show in the Park, already described. This was an exciting event for the whole village and everyone looked forward to it. In a huge marquee, the biggest I had ever seen, you smelt that immediately recognised smell of crushed green grass. Here flowers, cakes, jam and vegetables were displayed along with various craft items, and we were immensely proud when my mother won a prize for her cakes.

The school children joined enthusiastically in the Fancy Dress Parade, men skittled for a pig, the owners of rabbits and poultry exhibited their prize specimens in cages all up the drive and it felt like carnival time as the glorious rum-te-tum brass band boomed out over the Vale.

The event was held among the sloping, grass covered mounds above the foundations of Robert Boyle the scientist's original house, mounds that all the little girls rolled down enthusiastically.

Haymaking and The Flower Show were followed by harvest and in Dorset the wheat was hyled – put in hyles or sheaves in clumps, heads facing inwards to dry. At Sunday School we children used to sing a chorus which I particularly loved.

> 'Lift up your eyes and look on the fields
> Lift up your eyes and look on the fields.
> They're white already to harvest
> White already to harvest
> Pray ye therefore the Lord of the Harvest
> Pray ye therefore the Lord of the Harvest
> That he may send forth labourers
> Into His Harvest.

Sadly, when the war came the harvest fields were put down to new strains of wheat and firmly labelled on wooden notices on posts standing in the fields: 'Dorset War Agricultural Executive Committee Winter Sown Wheat Fields'. Try putting that mouthful into a tuneful Sunday School chorus, though Jennie and I did try.

Usually in the autumn, after the long hours of hard work in the fields were finished and (perhaps) there was a little spare money in pockets, the fair came to the village. There was a traditional fair ground beside the Methodist Chapel and excitement ran high as, first, curious machines and large vehicles arrived. Then roundabouts were set up, with wooden horses and garishly painted dragons, with flaring nostrils and somewhat vacant expressions.

The stalls of the fair often called for country people's skills – shooting and throwing especially. You shot at Aunt Sally and you shied up to three balls in each round at a row of coconuts set up in deep cups on stands in a row. I went to the fair with Mary and a young man and I longed for a coconut, though I couldn't throw for toffee. The young man gallantly said he would try for me. He shied with deadly accuracy and was rewarded with a lovely hairy coconut, which he immediately gave to me.

I was absolutely delighted and as soon as we got it home Mary drilled a hole in the coconut, drained out the milk and gave some to me. It was sweet and white, tasting quite unlike any milk I'd ever had before. The chewy white flesh was equally exciting and I envied children who lived on tropical islands where coconuts fell down like windfall apples.

Harvest time always seemed to me to be the climax of the year's seasons. There was, of course, harvest festival in church and in all the chapels to prove it. Hymns of thanksgiving were sung with feeling, whatever the harvest had been like, and the harvest supper and concert followed within a few days.

The valleys, said one of the Psalms, dropped fatness, so, in the Blackmore Vale, did the hedges. Hedging, the art of proper hedge laying, was a country skill greatly valued and widely practised in those days. The village of Stalbridge is mentioned in the Domesday Book, so no doubt many of the hedges were very old indeed. Modern hedges, that is to say, hedges that had been laid some one hundred and fifty years before, when the commons were enclosed, were easily recognised. They were dead straight and full of nothing but hawthorn, but the traditional old hedges, lovingly tended and laid for seven hundred years, were exceptionally fine and varied. They bore great crops of blackberries and my father always knew where to find the best. We picked them enthusiastically and the chestnut walking stick he always carried was invaluable for hooking down the high branches where the fruit was always the best.

The autumn hedges were a wonderful sight. Their primary purpose of course was to keep the stock in, so careful laying over the years thickened them impenetrably, protecting blackberry bushes and encouraging them to flourish. High up in those rich hedges clematis, which we called old man's beard, romped all over them and ripe orange hips and red haws gave colour to the whole.

7

Being Poorly

I CAME HOME from school one afternoon and found my mother occupied with a dark-haired young woman whom I vaguely remembered seeing about the village somewhere. They were talking earnestly, at least my mother was, and the young woman was crying.

'Why?' I thought irritably, do they always have to come and cry in our kitchen? 'Why can't they just go and cry somewhere else?' It was a fruitless question. Young women always came to my mother to pour out their troubles. She was that sort of person.

When my mother had been left at the age of twenty with her two younger sisters and her father to care for, all her girlhood hopes of a nursing career faded. She would have loved to be a nurse and Gloucester, where she lived, had a greatly respected Infirmary. She could have trained there, but she had no chance. So she did a lot of home nursing, including assisting the midwife at home births, and became advisor, confidante and substitute mother to everybody around her in the village.

The young woman was worried about her baby. It cried all the time. I thought all babies cried all the time, but it seemed, from what my mother was saying, that they really had a whole lot of different cries and that each could mean something different.

My mother kissed me and told me I could have the two pieces of bread and butter that were covered up between two plates on the dresser, but nothing else as it would soon be teatime. Oh no, it wouldn't. From the way the young mother was going on, crying and sniffing and describing the baby's revolting practices in disgusting detail, tea wouldn't be ready for ages.

My mother put the kettle on and went on with what she was saying, only the kettle would be for a good strong cup of tea for the weeping willow, not us. All the weeping willows got disgustingly strong tea in our house.

'It cheers them up and steadies their nerves,' my mother would say. Well, from the way this one was going on she'd need the urn from the Parish Room.

'There's no such thing as temper in a young baby,' my mother continued. 'If he cries he's uncomfortable. Perhaps his binder is too tight, or you put it on just before his feed. If you do that, then give him a good meal, the binder constricts the full stomach.'

'What's a binder?' I asked with my mouth full. Mother explained that it was a sort of crepe bandage that went round the baby's middle to support it, fastened with a safety pin. It sounded worse than stays. Old people in the village wore stays, other grown ups wore corsets and some girls in my class wore liberty bodices though my mother had never insisted on them for me, except in cold weather, thank goodness.

'Babies aren't really all that breakable you know.' Mother went on. 'They need careful, gentle handling, of course. Support his head and mind the fontanelle.'

'What's the fontanelle?' I wanted to know. My mother looked at me.

'It's the soft bit on the baby's head where the bones haven't quite closed over.' She said.

The kettle boiled but instead of getting up to make the tea my mother went on looking at me. I knew what that look meant. I swallowed the last bit of bread and butter and went upstairs, leaving them to it. When I left, my mother was recommending boracic powder. As I closed the kitchen door behind me I heard the young mother ask about his motions, which were loose. Oh, I knew what that meant. Filthy little beast.

Mother appeared to know such a lot abut people's health, sometimes she seemed to know about their illnesses before they happened. There were times when I would hear her prophesy to my father.

'I saw Fred Harrison this morning, Arthur,' I heard her say once. 'He looked so pale and he had dark shadows under his eyes. I should never be surprised to hear there's a bit of kidney trouble there.'

Next year she was proved right. Fred Harrison went into hospital on account of his kidneys. This sort of thing kept happening. My mother's health forecasts were forever coming true. It was all very strange.

The grown ups did seem to think a lot about illness. Once upstairs I inspected my mother's array of remedies. Vaseline, thick yellow stuff in glass jars, seemed to be everywhere. So was Germolene. Two large tins of it, a pretty shade of pink with a hot, pungent smell. We put it on cuts and grazes and it made them feel better at once. Then there were the tinctures, tincture of arnica for sprains and bruises and tincture of iodine for cuts. Iodine stung terribly. I made much more fuss about the prospect of iodine than I did about the cut, so I usually managed to avoid having it applied.

To the right of these bottles there was a group of medicines a bit separate from the others. 'Cascara' I read, a thick, sticky, black liquid. The label then went on about 'chronic congestion of the bowels' so it was obvious what that was for. My mother always kept it but she did not insist on dosing her daughters with it every Saturday night, whether they had need of it or not. One of my friends' mothers did that, at the same time regaling her with horrific tales about the brimstone and treacle with which she had been dosed by her own mother when young.

The medicine cupboard also contained a large bottle marked 'Californian Syrup of Figs' and a packet of 'Finest Dried Senna Pods,' from which my mother was sometimes known to make a witches brew of evil looking liquid for some poor old soul in the neighbourhood.

Most of the medicines were in fluted glass bottles, clear usually, brown if poisonous or sometimes blue or dark green. I suppose the nine green bottles hanging on the wall all looked like that. These bottles had corks in them, rather musty smelling corks. Then a glass-stoppered bottle caught my eye. This was in thick glass but rather nicely cut in a graceful shape. It was a quite different green from the bottle green, a sort of bright, light emerald coloured, and I suddenly remembered what it was. It was a bottle of smelling salts that had belonged to old Aunt Em. In her last years she sometimes let me have a sniff from the smelling bottle. It was supposed to clear the head and revive the sniffer, particularly in case of faintness. When I was five I felt it was going to blow my head off. Now I was nearly eight it simply made me sneeze violently.

I rubbed my eyes and nose with the back of my hand and put the smelling salts back beside a large cream-coloured bottle marked 'Embrocation for Horses and Cattle'.

'This celebrated embrocation,' I read, 'should be in the possession of all farmers and owners of stock. It is invaluable for wounds, lacerations, bruises, hard swellings, sprains, stakes, curbs, sore back and broken knees.'

Well, if tea wasn't ready soon I was going downstairs to suggest horse liniment for the baby. This horse liniment had always been highly regarded in my family and it really was effective. As my mother remarked, if it could penetrate a racehorse's knees, it would probably do wonders for a bad back. The liniment was cream coloured, easily rubbed in and a lot less smelly than the other medicaments. 'The Embrocation' for instance, which stood next to it had been 'put up' by either the local chemist or my parents' favourite firm of herbalists, and I remembered that when my father had a bad back it stank the house out. We could smell it for some time after it was no longer being used. It seemed to permeate the very walls.

Wintergreen, in a big brown pot, stood next to the

embrocation. It was a thick, sticky ointment, deep black in colour but overlaid with a sort of thick dark green, like the moss that grew inside the well at Thornhill or old Mr. Antell's Sunday hat. Wintergreen stank too, and made an awful mess.

There didn't seem to be much in the medicine chest for my needs, but then I didn't get much wrong with me. I could dimly remember chicken pox and having to stay at home from school for three weeks. Some children had their hands tied at night so that they could not pick the spots and get a scar, but I was spared that. Measles, which for me was still to come, meant being really ill and feverish and, in bad cases, lying in a darkened room for days, as the virus could damage the eyes. I was lucky, I didn't get measles badly. Jennie got it, also mildly, after I did, which was fun in a way, as I was able to visit her and read her excellent supply of comics (out loud to her of course),unless she looked tired. Then I read quietly to myself.

The only thing I could find in the medicine chest for me was an old bottle of cocaine and oil of cloves to put on aching teeth. I had toothache quite badly once at the age of five. My mother said it was the herbal tablets. These were sticky oblong sweets of a deep yellow colour and a lovely aromatic herbal flavour. My father was devoted to them and carried a cone shaped paper bag of them everywhere. Every night when he came to say goodnight, he would produce the sticky bag and we would have a herbal tablet apiece, sucking them companionably. Then he would go, leaving me to finish mine and drift off to sleep.

My teeth had, of course, already been cleaned and my prayers said, and the harm the herbal tablets was doing to them simply did not occur to my affectionate father. I had a sort of gut feeling that it would be better if I did not mention it to my mother, but all too soon I developed decay in my back teeth and my mother, as ever, worked the matter out for herself. Herbal tablets were forbidden for evermore once my teeth had been cleaned.

I lay in bed on the night of the edict feeling miserable that such a pleasant custom should have come to an abrupt end, when suddenly there was a familiar rustle of sticky paper bag and a voice saying 'Here you are, my child, the very last one, and don't tell your mother.' We hugged our secret and never told a soul.

The result of my toothache was that my mother dabbed the teeth with a compound of cocaine and oil of cloves to deaden the pain. When she went out of the room and left the bottle on the mantelpiece, I decided that my teddy bear had toothache, so I nipped out of bed and dabbed his snout with the sticky brown mixture. The marks stayed there, ineradicably, on his furry face.

My mother's voice calling from downstairs that tea was ready interrupted my rummaging. The young mother had finally gone, looking much happier.

'What that poor Mrs. Wells needs,' my mother remarked over tea, 'is a bit more practical help from her mother-in-law, which she might get if the old girl didn't spend all her time gossiping with the neighbours. And she needs a good tonic too.'

In saying this, my mother had put her finger unerringly on two major aspects of village life, gossip and the need everyone had of tonics. They were both, in my mother's mind, medical matters.

Gossip occupied a great deal of time in the village, especially among women. There were few strange faces in the village streets. When any appeared, enquiries were instantly made, and circulated, about who they were, so everyone was well known and their activities and business observed and recorded. This meant reputation was of tremendous importance. Women who valued their reputation would think twice before going into any of the village's four public houses with their husbands. Pubs were essentially a male preserve. And as for going into them alone, well, any woman who did that in our village lost every shred of 'character' she might once have had.

The suggestion that a married woman was 'carrying on' with

another man set tongues wagging ferociously, and the offender (at any rate the female offender) was soon made aware of public censure. There had, in times past, been the famous Skimmity Ride when 'respectable' people in the village would make an effigy of the guilty couple and parade it through the streets, banging saucepans together and shouting as they went. The last Skimmity Ride in our village had been planned at a house called Silk Hay in the High Street, a medieval hall house with a sixteenth century extension in front, on the corner of Silk House Barton. The family who lived there then knew a married woman was 'carrying on' and felt it would be a great joke to organise a Skimmity Ride, so they made the effigies and collected pots and pans and stored them in the nearby donkey house, while they recruited participants. All this had been a mere thirty years ago. In fact, that Skimmity Ride never took place as the police got to hear of it and stopped it, but an intense interest in scandal and women's extramarital activities had been a feature of village life ever since. I noticed that scandalous stories often grew in the telling, and any activity by anyone, however innocent, always acquired an immoral construction, wherever possible. My mother, though, saw the whole matter of scandal as a medical problem.

'It's all the intermarriage in the past before the railways came, Arthur, and nobody could find a wife outside the village,' she would declare firmly to my father. 'That's what's caused all this scandal mongering. An obsession with other people's morals is always a sign of mental disorder, and you get that from too much inbreeding.'

'True, oh Queen,' my father would reply. It was his usual remark at such times, and probably the safest.

My mother understood the nature of gossip and she understood equally well that tonics were things everybody needed. She did not subscribe to the school of thought that said a tonic must taste nasty or it would not do any good, though she knew this was a view widely held in the village. But a tonic with a pleasant taste, bright, red, probably full of iron, and supplied by the doctor to his panel patients who needed it, was, my mother felt, an extremely sensible course of action. A tonic full of vitamins and minerals might well be able to make up for what a frugal diet lacked, or it might have the equally invaluable therapeutic effect of making the patients feel they were doing something to help themselves and so worry less about their health.

If, as happened surprisingly often, local people did not wish to go to the doctor, either because they never had, or because of a superstitious dread of what he might tell them, then my mother would recommend tonic foods. There was a surprising number of these available from the village chemist. Alternatively my mother would recommend nourishing dishes from the 'Invalid Cookery' section of her favourite cookery book. This book had been published in 1927. It was called *The Radiation Cookery Book* and was intended for users of the Radiation New World oven with 'Regulo' Automatic Heat Controller (a huge innovation then). My mother did not have this cooker, or cook by gas, but she appreciated the traditional Englishness of the recipes. I enjoyed reading the book. It told you how to make things called 'Beef Tea' and 'Chicken Quenelles' and 'Cow-heel Jelly' or 'Gruel'. It sounded a bit like black magic.

If my mother thought their purses could stand it, she would suggest tonic wine. There were several well-known brands of this, all of them a bright shade of ruby red. Tonic wine had one great social advantage in our village – it was perfectly respectable. The village was predominantly Liberal voting and therefore tee-total (there was a connection there – brewers were Tories) but tonic wine was bought and drunk openly and no-one was criticised for it.

Sometimes my mother would recommend a herbalist who held consultations in the Salvation Army hall in Yeovil. This herbalist was an old friend. He had begun theological studies years before with my mother's brother Tom, with a view to entering the Congregational Ministry, but had given it up to be a herbalist. My mother occasionally consulted him about her own health whose problems were thought to stem from the severe and debilitating attack of scarlet fever she had contracted when I was five.

This herbalist prescribed herbal medicines, which did taste foul. They generally looked horrible, black or brown in colour with a tendency to settle, producing a thick sediment and needing to be shaken vigorously. Yet the curious thing was that my mother, totally free from Puritanical notions about only nasty things being effective, brought these murky looking bottles home and took the medicine religiously as prescribed. I never quite understood this ambivalence of hers about medicines.

In fact, my mother was fascinated by herbs and herbal remedies, as her own mother had been, and she sometimes sent to a well-known firm of herbalists for remedies in which she had faith. Once when Mary became rather spotty in adolescence, my mother declared firmly that her blood was out of order, and sent for some 'Blood Purifying Herbs'. These had to be made into a drinkable infusion by pouring boiling water on to several tablespoons of the herbs in a big jug, then leaving it to stand all day. The smell was most peculiar – bitter and herby and slightly fusty, like mildewed hay. Mary said the taste was unbelievably vile and she held her nose between finger and thumb firmly and dramatically to get each draught down. The herbs worked, though, and all her spots cleared up.

A lot of ailments in the village related to work. Colds and chills were common and often the result of getting soaking wet through getting cows in, and having to stay wet while they were milked. Coughs often developed as the result of chills and these, if they were racking or persistent, caused great alarm. Tuberculosis had been a scourge in the village in times past and many families including my own were known to have had a history of TB. The germs had often come from cows, and one tubercular, emaciated beast was enough to infect the whole herd's yield.

Tubercular testing and immunisation of cows was beginning to be known in the dairy farming Blackmore Vale, but there were still cases of TB of the lungs from infected cows' milk, and of children with tubercular limbs. A famous children's hospital in Bath had many such young children with TB of the hips and other joints. Jennie's mother caught the disease from her brother who was a milk recorder and was thought to have picked it up from a cow. The brother died from it. He was a man of about forty years old with a wife and a little girl.

While he was still able to drive he one day took his daughter and Jennie and me out for a ride. We sat in the back of the little Austin Seven and I occasionally caught sight in the driving mirror of his unnaturally bright brown eyes and pale, hollow cheeks.

Jennie's mother recovered from TB. She had to go into a sanatorium for a year's rest and treatment among pine trees. My mother explained that the pine trees gave off healing properties and by resting in bed there she would be well again. Jennie and her father were looked after by her grandparents who lived next door, and her mother eventually made a complete recovery. The saddest thing, to my mind, though, was that Jennie's beautiful long brown hair had to be cut short – her grandmother could not cope with putting it up in rags to make ringlets every night.

In our village bad backs were extremely common. This could result from such things as lifting a sack of meal awkwardly, or falling, especially losing one's footing beside the slippery gutter of a cowstall, and going down with a crack on its stone floor. The other threat to village backs was lumbago, for which the only real cures were rest and warmth, both difficult to come by if the sufferer was the village milkman or a farm labourer. Time off work was avoided, unless it was impossible for the sufferer to carry on, because unemployment or sickness pay was very low, and the only other source of maintenance was payment from a friendly society such as The Rechabites – a temperance based society which my father belonged to.

This meant bad backs had to be cured by homely remedies. A piece of flannel, red flannel my mother said was best, was stitched into the undergarments of the victim, so that it was stretched firmly across the affected part. Another remedy was to fix a piece of brown paper across the sufferer's back, warm the flat iron against the bars of the range or fire, taking care that it did not get too hot, then iron the brown paper. The heat was very soothing. So was an earthenware hot water bottle or a warm brick, though both were a bit hard.

In our family when anyone had lumbago, my mother, who had marvellous rubbing fingers, rubbed in the various embrocations, including horse liniment. Homely remedies were used for other ailments besides bad backs. Goose grease saved from a Christmas goose would be warmed and rubbed into the chest to ease a tight cough. The middle of a raw onion, sometimes rubbed lightly with camphorated oil would be placed in the ear of a child suffering with earache, to ease the pain by its warmth. In cases of bronchitis an old black kettle would be put on the fire and left to boil, to moisten the atmosphere and make breathing easier for the patient.

Many illnesses required careful nursing and a great deal of skill and judgement. An experienced nurse was a perfect treasure in a village like ours, and in some types of illness the survival of the patient related directly to the skill of the nurse. Pneumonia was one such complaint. The patients' fever raged uncontrollably, making them hotter and hotter, and great care had to be taken in any methods used to try to cool them. They could be sponged and the bed clothes adjusted a bit, but in the end the illness had to come to a crisis. The dreadful colour and laboured breathing had to be watched and monitored until either the fever raged uncontrollably and the doomed died before the eyes of the horrified watchers, or they passed the crisis, the breathing became quieter and more normal and weeks of devoted nursing led to a gradual recovery.

As well as a district nurse, the village always had at least one hard-working, good-hearted woman who would sit up at night beside the sick and dying to give the regular nurse or watcher a rest. Then when the end came, she would lay out the deceased. I remembered this from Aunt Em's death when I was six, for it meant preparing the corpse to look as pleasant as possible in its coffin before the relatives came in to take a last look and the coffin was screwed down. Taking a last look had almost a social significance and close friends and relations who lived near came in to pay their respects.

Many illnesses, though, fortunately ended in recovery. An illness of my father's at around my eighth birthday ended well, and for me in exceptionally happy circumstances. My father had contracted a severe chill which brought about pulmonary inflammation and serious debility. This was viewed very gravely by our doctor, who knew of the family's respiratory history. When June came and my father had still not recovered his strength, the doctor insisted that he must go away to the seaside for a complete change of air. My father was appalled. He had never been to the sea at all, except for an occasional day's outing. And as for going away from home without his family, for that is what it would mean, nothing that could happen to him could possible depress him more. However, the doctor insisted, so arrangements were made for him to spend three weeks at Weymouth with a former Congregational minister from Stalbridge and his wife, Mr. and Mrs. Harris, who had retired there.

We could not all go. The Harrises had no room for us all, and anyway, it would have been too expensive, so there was nothing else for it. My wan and disconsolate father had to go by himself. Well before a week was up he wrote to my mother to say that he could not bear to be away from us, or the village, and unless she could join him there, he would come home. My worried mother knew that the visit to Weymouth was essential, but she could not leave Mary and me. So the most marvellous compromise was reached. It was decided that I should go. I was to have two weeks off from school and go to Weymouth to sleep in Mrs. Harris's tiny little spare room and keep my father company. Because it was term, Miss Pearse's consent had to be sought. She gave it readily enough, knowing the circumstances, and I went off with my mother by charabanc, feeling excited but a little over-awed.

Mr. and Mrs. Harris were quiet, kind, elderly people who seemed to be delighted to have a little girl in the house, and promptly taught me their address in case I got lost. Weymouth in the 1930's was a sedate seaside town, ideal for family holidays. It was full of young couples with children and often nursemaids, in or out of uniform, and the bathing was quite safe.

I could not swim yet, but I was a tadpole of a child and had brought my swimming things – a long, two-coloured swim suit with built up shoulders, an old towel and a bright red rubber bathing cap that smelt like the inner tube of a bicycle tyre. The sands stretched for what seemed like mile after golden mile, and every morning as soon as my breakfast had fairly 'gone down' I was in the sea.

The red bathing cap was a safety device. My father sat on a seat up on the front. He lacked energy still and could not face walking over the fine, dry sand for fear it might irritate his lungs. So he allowed me to go off to the sea alone, provided I wore the red bathing cap the whole time and promised to come in from the sea and straight back to him whenever I received a message to do so. This meant that every morning after I had had a really good bathe a different strange child would appear beside me in the water saying, 'There's a man up there on that seat and he says you've got to go in now.'

In the afternoons we would walk along the Backwater or

through fields towards Radipole and sometimes the girl next door, Brenda, who was a little older than me, would come with us. She was a well brought up girl, and when we got home she would say gravely to my father, 'Thank you for taking me.' I was very impressed by such self assurance.

One day my mother's second brother, Uncle Phil, and his wife came to spend the day with us and my mother found a charabanc outing from the village so she could come to Weymouth too. Uncle Phil had no children of his own and was by temperament endlessly patient, so we had a glorious afternoon making sand castles and digging holes, while my father sat on his usual seat on the front and read the paper or waved it towards us in friendly greeting. I tucked my frock in my knickers and Uncle Phil rolled his longjohns up over his trousers so that he could paddle effectively in the sea when it was his turn to fill the water bucket, and we remained absorbed until it was time for the visitors to leave.

One day I had a donkey ride on the sands on a quiet old donkey named Pop, and on another afternoon we went to Upwey to the Wishing Well there. This time we travelled in an open horse drawn bus, and on each occasion I wore an enormous, cream-coloured broad-brimmed panama hat. A similar hat, though larger, I noticed was worn by my father. People seemed to regard hats as exceptionally important and anyway the sun striking the beach and esplanade was very hot. There was, we knew, a woman in the village who had got sunstroke one hot day in her youth and never recovered enough to leave her room ever again.

The holiday greatly improved my father's health and I too, perfectly fit when we started, became browner and fitter looking with every day. Eventually, the companionable, busy two weeks came to an end. We packed our old fashioned suitcases and said goodbye to Mr. and Mrs. Harris. 'Thank you for having me,' I said gravely and I thought they looked impressed.

When we got home, bursting with excitement, or at least I was, to tell my mother every detail of the journey, we went straight into the kitchen. My mother looked pleased to see us and blew me a kiss, but she could not get out of her chair. On her lap she held The Baby, the one that had come before when it was tiny. It was a fat, ill-tempered looking monster now. In her free hand she was holding a thick, banana shaped glass feeding bottle. It had a thick brown rubber teat at one end and a piece of thick, flat, rubber at the other. Goodness knows why that was there, even this baby could hardly suck from both ends.

My mother was talking to the dark haired young mother who, I saw at once, looked happier and more relaxed now.

'I expect you'll find he'll do well with this,' my mother was saying soothingly. 'I'm sorry your milk has failed, but now he's past three months it's time to start mixed feeding anyway.' She put the creature against her shoulder where it made the most disgusting belch.

'Don't worry,' my mother said cheerfully, smiling at the young woman. 'Babies are astonishingly tough little creatures.' I caught my breath sharply and my mother glanced at me inquiringly. I had been about to remark that this one looked as tough as an old boot.

8

Being Different

THE VILLAGE, I soon realized, was full of 'characters'. The coming of the railway in the 1860's had brought change but the size and shape of the village, along with its buildings, had remained unchanged for generations. The houses, cottages, shops, workshops and farms had often been lived in and used for several generations by the same family as tenants of the Stalbridge Estate on a monthly, Quarter Day or Annual Lady Day tenancy. Members of the Westminster family (surnamed Grosvenor) had acquired considerable estates in Dorset during the 19th century, first Motcombe in 1825 and Stalbridge in 1854. The estates had been well looked after and were profitable.

In 1886 Lord Richard d'Aquila Grosvenor had been created Baron Stalbridge. He had been caught up in unforeseen financial difficulties but had been able, through stringent economies, to pass the estate to his son Lord Hugh Grosvenor, the second Baron. This Lord Stalbridge has spent his early years in the Army, rejoining it in 1914. His marriage had not been happy and he decided, before hostilities ceased, to sell his Shaftesbury and Stalbridge estates. His son was killed in a flying accident in 1930 so the Stalbridge Barony ended.

The decision to sell the Stalbridge Estate in September 1918 meant that many village families had the chance to buy the property they had rented for years.

This chance to buy, coupled with gloving offering opportunities for women and girls, reinforced the natural independence of the people. Gloving had for years been a source of income for women and girls who would otherwise have been dependent on their husbands and fathers. Yeovil was the gloving town of the area and is still well-known for its leather industry, but a well organized system of piece work covered the district round. Fine leather gloves were greatly in demand and the women and girls of some Stalbridge families were capable of exquisite sewing. The work of Stalbridge glove-maker Miss Jessie Webber is now featured in the Dorset County Museum.

It was perhaps the less skilled who used a treadle sewing machine – by which output was increased. The Revd. W S Swayne, a curate at Stalbridge in the 1880's and later Bishop of Lincoln, observed 'If a mother tried to control her daughter, the girl was apt to say "I will take my machine and go elsewhere."' This ingrained independence meant that some people simply did not conform to what society expected of them, and for other reasons – health, upbringing and heredity – they were different.

One of these independent spirits was to be seen taking the air on Post Office Corner in the daytime (in the evening this spot was where the boys waited for the girls). His name was George North and he would stand on the corner, an extremely grimy figure in a black overcoat with string round it. He carried a knobby stick and stood on the pavement outside the Post Office, feet astride and holding the stick away from him, as if daring anyone to come too close. His eyes were bright and belligerent in his dirty face and I always felt he had a score to settle with life. I didn't discover what it was – nobody seemed to know.

People were good to George. Mr. and Mrs. Herbert Parsons opposite gave him a meal every day and at Christmas they gave him a full Christmas dinner and beer. My mother would pack up my father's discarded shirts and underwear into a brown paper parcel bound with thick string. Then she would label it in her neat handwriting 'George North. The Post Office.'

'How will he know the things are there?' I asked anxiously.

'Oh, the Postmaster will give them to him,' my mother replied. 'Everybody knows George North.'

Sometimes it was a name that made people seem different, to me at any rate. Take Witty Haskett. He was an exceptionally lively man, full of jokes and apt retorts to everyone he met, and I supposed that he was called Witty because he was witty. I heard people all around me laughing at his jokes. It was only after his death that I learned his name was Gideon Whitfield Haskett, so he was really Whitty.

Charley Everett was different too. My mother said he was 'simple' which was a good word to use of him. He walked simply up and down Jarvis field every summer evening, all the evening, just walking along the same path by the hedge. Sometimes little groups of children would follow him, then draw level with him, teasing him a bit. After a while Charley would pretend to grab the nearest child and they would all run shrieking away. Charley was quite harmless and these encounters were enjoyed by both sides.

One woman in the village I dearly loved was Emily Gatehouse, the stepdaughter of Mrs. Gatehouse of Snowdon House where we lived when we first moved up to the village. She must have been nearly sixty when I got to know her. She had a mental age of not a great deal more than my own age of seven and she was epileptic. Not much was or could be done about it. Most of the time she was free of fits and seemed well and energetic. This meant that she passed as a grown up and I was allowed to go out for walks whenever I wished, as long as Emily was with me. Poor Emily. We scrambled around muddy ditches and river banks, anywhere that interested me. Once we found a spot where a tramp had evidently lain up the night before. Emily never seemed to mind where we went. She was shabby and neglected and had been put upon as a drudge all her life, so to have a friend of her own, even if it was a bossy little girl of seven was, I think, a treat for her.

Her fits came on when the moon changed or was full, which meant that old Mrs. Gatehouse would mark up the religiously inclined almanack on the dresser and know when to expect them. My mother, too, was on the alert at these times, though I did not realize this until one of Emily's fits came on. We were sitting at the kitchen table in her end of the house, Emily and I, her old stepmother watching us beadily from the fireside, as we played with a cardboard game of mine. Suddenly she looked at me with glazed eyes and seemed to stutter.

'Come quick, t'is her time on her!' I heard the old lady shout to my mother in the garden.

Emily went stiff. Her fingers and thumb closed on the cardboard game in an iron grip, wrenching it from its base, and all the rough skin and white creases between the potato stains on her work worn hands stood out in sharp relief against her white knuckles.

I was very quickly taken out of the kitchen with murmured assurances.

'Emily's not very well. She'll be better soon. She can come out with you again next week, you'll see.'

My mother's voice was calm and firm. When I next saw Emily a week later, she was her usual, happy, simple-minded, good-natured self.

Emily died one cold winter day several years after we left Snowdon House. The Congregational Minister Mr. Davidson held a simple funeral service for her in the front room, the old drawing room of the house. The large, framed, sepia photograph of Percy Gatehouse looked down on us and the long, white, Victorian lace curtains rustled, breathing gently against the wall. It was all just as it had always been.

Another woman I knew slightly named Jeans was epileptic and, like Emily, nothing much could be done for her. The little cottage where she lived had burnt down early one morning in circumstances that were never really explained. She went into lodgings for a bit, but then it was said that 'she would have to be put away.'

Put Away! Cold dread gripped me. It sounded so final. What did it mean? My mother was always telling me to put things away, usually when I had my nose in a book. By this she meant putting them away in drawers or in a dark cupboard. Surely nothing like that was going to happen to Miss Jeans? Again, I did what I always did when confronted with circumstances I did not understand – I asked my mother what it meant.

'It's just an expression people use,' she said gently. 'It means she will go to live in a place near Charminster where she will be looked after. She will like it there, I'm sure.'
My mother sounded just a little too anxious to be reassuring and I was still worried.

'When will she come home?' I wanted to know. It was my mother's turn to look anxious.

'She won't be coming home,' she said in the same gentle voice. 'You see, she can't look after herself. She really isn't well enough. It's the best thing for her.'

My mother, who knew she was dealing with a child prone to nightmares, had succeeded in calming my fears. I thought no more about it until the following summer when we went to Weymouth on a rare outing. We went in the direction of the County Asylum near Charminster and on a quiet country road we passed a crocodile of patients. They were walking slowly in the sunshine, some absolutely silent, others talking and laughing, perhaps rather excitedly. Some of them were rather oddly dressed with unmatched clothes in bright colours, but they were clean and well cared for. My mother smiled at me. We did not mention our Miss Jeans but she was in our thoughts.

Sometimes children were different because they were what was usually called 'simple'. Our indomitable headmistress Miss Pearse took the view that if a child taught by her methods could not read and write by the age of just over seven, then something was lacking in the child. Very occasionally, she was able to find a place in a special school suited to its needs.

Before Miss Pearse's arrival little had been done to help children who were backward or had learning difficulties. My parents knew of one such girl, barely able to write her name, who was obliged to attend the village school till the age of fourteen, simply because the law said she had to. She may have learned some elements of domestic work there, as she later turned out to be good at simple household tasks: most of the time though when she attended the village schools she was bored and unhappy.

Sometimes babies were born in the village who were normal but not very strong or bright because, my mother insisted, the blame lay with 'the gloving and that treadle'. Naturally, I wanted to know what a treadle was and my mother explained that although gloves were often stitched by hand sometimes the glover used a treadle machine. This had a flat plane at an angle underneath it that had to be worked with the foot in order to power the machine. The constant use of the foot by a pregnant woman must, my mother insisted, affect the baby, no doubt reducing it wits and causing it to be puny.

Gloving was an important occupation in a village like ours, giving women a vitally necessary addition to the family's income as well as much valued independence. It was the boast of some married women that by 'sticking at it' they could earn as much as their husbands. Every week they would take their finished work to the distributor (usually at a house in the High Street) to have it checked and paid for. The money was then entirely theirs and they would go away with next week's consignment of cut skins.

Gloving though could not be considered a healthy occupation. It necessitated long hours sitting over a needle, doing fine work, or using the hand or foot repetitively to work a machine. The hunched position of the worker eventually produced round shoulders or, much more seriously, a persistent cough. There were girls from some families my mother was convinced would have been better if they had gone away to service. Then perhaps they might have met husbands from completely different bloodlines.

Sometimes people in the village were different because they were dreamy and artistic. One of these was Allan Parsons, a childhood friend of my father. The two young men had once gone to London by train but, country boys at heart, they did not like it and never went again.

Allan, the only child of a baker, was trained by his father as a master baker. The work suited him and with his artistic nature he excelled at delicately icing cakes. The business flourished as long as his parents were alive, but after his mother's death he was not businesslike enough to cope with it, and it declined. Allan took up barbering, equipping himself with a set of barbers' tools and some suitable chairs. He became a good barber but slow. Allan dearly loved a gossip and the kettle was always on for tea.

The story goes that a small boy was sent by his mother straight from school to Allan to get his hair cut. When the boy had not returned two hours later his irate mother arrived to take him home as tea was on the table. The child's hair was half cut by then, but his mother bore him away just the same and sent him back the next day to be finished.

Allan continued to shave and cut hair in his shop. His deft, steady hands inspired confidence and he would shave selected customers, especially invalids, in their own home. On occasions he was sent for to shave the rector. Allan knew his Bible and took great delight in quoting a verse from scripture, then looking at the lather covered rector expectantly to see if he would cap the quotation – which he always could.

Allan was gentle, kind and even-tempered. His kindness extended to two old men, Jack and Charlie, who had fallen on hard times and no longer had anywhere to live. He took them both to live with him and they sat permanently by his fire, minding the tea kettle, until the quiet routine ended for them all. Allan had not asked much from life. After his one excursion to London with my father many years before, I doubt if he ever left the village again.

People in the village could also be different because of drink, or at any rate the excess of it. A cider barrel was often kept in the outhouse of farms and many smallholdings and cottages. Sometimes people with their own cider apple orchards made their own cider and a huge cider press was passed around the village at harvest time. Cider was wholesome and strong and many people in and around the village drank it in prudent moderation.

Some however, did not. Farmers, drovers and farm workers were, in some ways, encouraged to drink to excess by the way in which hotels and inns remained open all day 'For the accommodation of farmers on market days'. The result was that sometimes a farmer would be seen driving his shabby old car shakily home, his face flushed, his speech slurred and looking very different from the way I remembered seeing him the day before.

My father's family, being Congregationalists and firm supporters of the Liberal party, did not drink. My grandfather Henry was said, in his bachelor and Dorset Yeomanry days, to have been a wild youth – though he later reformed. My father, born in 1881, grew up all too aware of the evils of drink. He knew that there were eleven pubs and cider houses in the parish and that if a working man chose to spend his wages in them, then his wife and children went hungry.

His writing desk, flat topped and mahogany, which he had asked a local cabinetmaker to make for him after his father Henry had died in 1907, bears this out. The cabinet maker in question was extremely good at his job but my father knew that when he had money he spent it all on drink. The desk was made and delivered and my father was delighted with it but he refused to pay the man. Instead, he paid his wife in instalments over two years and her gratitude was intense.

When he was sixteen my father had signed the pledge, resolving never to touch alcohol in any form and later supporting the Independent Order of Rechabites, a friendly society for teetotallers. Once my mother criticized my father to a friend, a farmer's wife, who rounded on her at once with the words:

'Don't ever let me hear you utter a word of criticism of that good man. At least when he comes home you will always know what state he's going to be in, which is more than I can say.'

Thrift and abstinence were reinforced for many by the threat of the workhouse – ours was at Sturminster Newton. The workhouse system had been introduced in 1834 to discourage the 'able-bodied poor' from applying for parish relief by making it necessary for them to enter a workhouse to get it. This system was intended to be nothing more than a last resort for the totally destitute. Conditions were deliberately made worse than the lowest paid labourer could achieve. Over the years, conditions had generally become less harsh, but even so workhouses were hated and feared by the poor.

Even the threat of being forced to enter the workhouse carried the prospect of disgrace at the back of the minds of ordinary people. The result of this fear bred both intensive thrift and a fierce, belligerent 'you won't get me' type of independence. This was the 1930's, a time of acute depression and poverty in the country as well as in towns, but hard up people in our village went to tremendous lengths to conceal their difficulties.

Years later when I left the village and went to live in London I was not in the least shocked by the sight of prostitutes in the streets, but the sight of beggars openly begging in London streets appalled me. I had not believed it was possible for people to behave in such a way.

Sometimes people in the village were different because they were not very clean. Clothes for working and retired women had always been chosen for their hard wearing qualities and they were generally black or a similar dark colour. This meant they did not show the dirt and did not need to be washed. The clothes of working men had been chosen with the same hard wearing qualities in mind but, with men, the reek of unwashed body was often overlaid with the smell of cheap plug tobacco.

It had always been difficult in the village to keep clean. Water, in many places, was still not laid on. If a farm or cottage had its own well the inhabitants were spared having to trudge back and forth with buckets several times a day. They simply went outside, hooked a large iron hook onto an aluminium or zinc bucket, turned a handle beside the wellhead and carefully let the bucket down into the depths on the end of a stout chain. In summer you often had to let it down a long way into the well's echoing depths before you could fill it, then slowly wind the chain back round the roller and carry your water home.

Householders without their own well went to the village pump in their street. The pumps on The Ring and at the top of Station Road served many houses, while the pumps in Back Lane and at the bottom of Church Hill were more localized. At the top of Church Hill there was a spring that never ran dry. The water was very pure and had poured out of the ground for centuries. It came out of a pipe in the wall above an old stone trough and the traveller John Leland had remarked on it as he rode through the village in the sixteenth century, calling it 'a right goodly springe on the south side of the church waullyd about.'

In a house opposite the spring a mother had brought up her seven children and she, her husband or the older children had fetched every drop of water for the household from that spring. Water was not laid on to those houses until about 1930 to give employment during the Depression.

My seven-year-old nose was sharp and I was soon able to distinguish between the smell of unwashed hair, never washed body and never washed feet. These smells were all different. My parents, and most of the people we knew, firmly believed that cleanliness was next to godliness. It was some time before I realized that the people who did not wash were also following a family tradition. They avoided washing themselves and their clothes because their forebears did not wash and in their hearts they felt such practices were unhealthy.

9
Church and Chapel

WHEN I WAS four I was taken to Evensong at the Parish Church with my mother and Mary. The Church, dedicated to St. Mary, was at the top of a steep hill. Then you climbed up an even steeper hill to reach the porch, its main entrance. Evensong, with its singing and chanting, was perhaps a bit complicated for a four-year-old and my mother observed me closely. Outside the church I looked with shining eyes down the slope towards the beautiful Blackmore Vale spread out below. My mother noticed this.

'What did you think of it?' she asked.

'Wouldn't this be a good place for the Old Grid to go down?' I replied ecstatically.

The Old Grid was a contraption made by Mary and the big boys she played with, using the wheels from my cast off pram, a plank and a length of rope to steer it (after a fashion). Sometimes when Mary and the boys were in a good mood they would let me have a ride on it.

After church we would walk or cycle home, with me being given a lift on Mary's bicycle carrier, carefully looking out for glow worms. These fascinating little beetles emitted a shining, greenish light after dark and we found them every few yards on the verges of our deserted country roads.

My parents had met when my mother's brother Uncle Tom became the Congregational Minister in Stalbridge where my father's lifelong allegiance to the Congregational Church was unshakeable. Uncle Tom, with his wife and young daughter Phyllis, had come to live in the Manse in Gold Street during the

First World War. My mother, in need of a holiday from her war work in a munitions factory, came to stay with them and went to the evening service on her first Sunday, to hear her brother preach. My father, for many years a deacon and treasurer in the Chapel, and considered by his family to be a confirmed bachelor, determined to make her his wife and they were married in 1920 after the Great War had ended.

However, my mother's upbringing in a family of low church Anglicans had given her an abiding love of that Church, especially of its music and the beauty of its liturgy. The result of this mixture was that Mary and I were baptised and confirmed in the Church of England but also attended chapel with our parents as a matter of course. Many years were to go by before I realized that not everybody did that, nor were they at home in both traditions.

St. Mary's Church retained a few medieval features, the most striking being a cadaver effigy of a corpse in a shroud. He is painfully thin with his ribs sticking through his skin. I was never frightened of him though, just full of pity that his mother had not been a good cook and generally a bit more like mine. The church had a tower, much higher than all the other nearby squat-towered village churches. The reason for our tower's great height was that the Revd. Henry Boucher, who lived at Thornhill House, wished to be able to see it from there. So he paid for it. That was in 1868.

There was a Church of England Mission School at Poolstown, on the way to Thornhill. It had a house for a missioner (and family) and a long schoolroom with an altar at one end. Here a clergyman could give communion to the people of this scattered area, or the missioner could take Evensong and organize a Sunday School. My mother taught in the Sunday School and Mary and I attended it.

As soon as we came to live in the village I was enrolled in the Church's Sunday School, held in our day school. Jennie was already a member so I could not help enjoying it. We sang a lot and took part in action songs. Every Sunday we were given a picture to stick in a little postcard album. This might be anything from an illustration of a bible story to a scene entitled 'Christian Marriage' showing a bride and bridegroom at a wedding.

After Sunday School one of the teachers took us for a sedate walk around the village – little girls in their Sunday best frocks and hats (straw hats with ribbons in summer). Eventually, as soon as we were old enough, we went off for a walk on our own. Ours were very different. We scrambled though hedges and over streams where we washed the mud off our straw hats and hoped the damage to our best frocks would not show.

The church was lit by gas light and I was always particularly aware of the two gas lamps on a cast iron cross beam in the nave beside our pew. When the gas was turned on there was a terrific roaring sound in the gas mantles, then some brave soul lit the gas and light crept down over the waiting congregation. It was quite different from the way electric light instantly lit up the hairdressers' premises.

The Church's year acted as a trigger for many things. Shrove Tuesday signalled the beginning of Lent next day, but a festive tea with pancakes that night. Lent brought the yearly collection for the Waifs and Strays (now called the Church of England Children's Society). We were given flat purple collecting boxes to take home and put in any money we'd saved by giving up sweets for Lent.

Easter was lovely of course, with Good Friday afternoon spent picking primroses with my father to decorate the Church next day. Primroses like damp, mossy places but not too dim, and we knew from experience where to find the best, longest stemmed flowers and the fattest, greenest leaves. The old orchard in Stalbridge Park was the best place of all, but our choice was wide.

Next morning, with my primroses tied up with wool in small bunches ('Be sure to include plenty of leaves, dear'), I was assigned to an older girl in the Sunday School, and we would happily decorate the children's corner with its beautifully made little chairs, pictures and illustrated books. Perhaps our decorations did not quite live up to the good design around us, for our bunches of primroses were plonked into jam pots.

Rogation Days, with the blessing of the crops, and Lammastide, the offering of the first fruits of the harvest, brought special services and hymns, greatly appreciated in that farming valley. Local farmers, who were sometimes choirmen, were readily involved.

There always seemed to be something going on in connection with the Church during the summer. On Hospital Sunday gifts were brought to the altar and donated to the local hospital. The Sunday School children took their gifts in procession to the altar – Jennie's grandfather always gave her a basket of eggs . And with gifts of produce and money the hospital benefitted greatly. Our local hospital, the Yeatman Hospital at Sherborne, had been opened in 1866 in memory of the Revd. Harry Farr Yeatman, a greatly respected landowner from nearby Stock House. It had been added to over the years but was still small and was always considered a local treasure. Many local people paid into the Hospital Association, an insurance scheme against the cost of hospital treatment, which was organized by Mrs. Moyle, our doctor's wife.

One of the most popular events of the summer was the Mothers' Union Garden Party. Everyone dressed up a bit for this. It was held in the Rectory garden, with its rolling lawns and a beautiful blue cedar tree. It was mature and exceptionally lovely, probably planted when the Rectory was built in 1699. I realized early that only the best families had a cedar tree in the garden. There was only one other such tree in the parish and that was in the grounds of Thornhill House. It too had probably been planted when that house was built – by the painter Sir James Thornhill in about 1725.

At the end of July our church school broke up for the summer holidays and five lovely weeks stretched out in front of us. Soon after we broke up came the absolute highlight of my summer – the Sunday School outing to Weymouth. We – at any rate our parents – had paid into a fund for this all the year and finally the day itself arrived.

We travelled in a charabanc. Lovelace's 'sharry' picked us up by the market cross in the High Street. We all piled in, stowing our sandwiches and high shouldered one piece bathing costumes on the racks at high speed, in a fever to be off. The rector, Mr. Merriman, came to call the roll and wish us a good day. His two younger daughters Patricia and Anne were with him, neat and trim in sandals and shorts with matching blouses, ideal for a day on Weymouth sands with us. I was delighted for them, for to my mind, bossed about by their governess or away at boarding school, they never seemed to me to have such an interesting life as I did.

I smiled at them delightedly but they did not smile back. In fact, they looked a bit glum. Then the awful truth dawned on me. They weren't coming with us. They weren't going to paddle out into the bay over the ridges of warm sand as the tide went out. They weren't going to eat big cones of ice creams on the sand, or have donkey rides or buy one of those garish bakelite windmills on a stick. They weren't going to have a ride in a swinging boat – higher and higher as they held on to the thick gaudy safety strap like or a huge Victorian bell pull.

The rector said a few words and his daughters waved us off. I turned to my mother.

'They're not coming. The Merriman girls aren't coming with us.'

My voice was choked and my eyes were full of tears. My mother immediately recognized the symptoms of an over excited child.

'They're coming later.' She said firmly. 'Mr. Merriman is going to bring them down to Weymouth by car later on.'

I was perfectly satisfied with this answer and forgot all about them.

The seats of Lovelace's 'sharry' were upholstered in some kind of uncut hairy moquette but the scenery was too fascinating to wriggle about much. Eventually we reached Dorchester and the long avenue of trees that met overhead like a tunnel on the way to Weymouth. Then, past the Ridgeway, we could smell the sea and finally, we could see it. Shouts of 'The sea!' echoed through the charabanc.

Once established on the sands with my mother and some friends in deck chairs, I had absolutely no intention of being moved from the beach. After lunch my mother wanted to go and look at the shops. Shops! How could anybody with a day of enchantment to spend in and beside the sea, want to look at shops?

Eventually, after six o'clock the long, lovely day on the sands ended. We sang songs on the homeward coach and I sat very still, partly because I was tired but chiefly because Lovelace's uncut moquette upholstery was uncomfortable on my newly sunburned legs.

Harvest Festival, early in October, meant a riotously decorated church. The church seemed full of marrows and beans and sheaves of corn and trailing old man's beard. It had that special smell of the good earth that only comes to such a place at such a time, which, in our church, was heightened by the equally special smell of flaring gas mantles overhead. Later that week an enormous parish harvest tea was held in the Junior School and the harvest produce sold.

After Harvest Festival came Armistice Sunday and the procession of ex-servicemen along the High Street and up Church Hill to the War Memorial in the churchyard. I noticed then that some of the veterans limped badly. I saw them working in shops in the village – the fishmonger's for instance or repairing boots – but it was only when they walked through the village in the Armistice parade that I realized how badly they walked. It was many years before I realized that they had lost a leg or a foot or been gassed in the Great War.

We gathered round the War Memorial and the names of the dead were read out, far, far more young men than the village could spare. They were the sons, husbands and fathers of the people around me, and the playmates of the survivors who had just trudged up to the War Memorial. Percy Gatehouse of Snowdon House, Emily's half-brother, was one, Jennie's uncle Ivor Hopkins another, and sometimes a group of men with the same name was read out. Were they brothers I wondered? We kept silence in their memory, then Charlie Jeans took up his trumpet and the Last Post and Reveille rang out over the Vale.

Some activities connected with the Church went on all through the winter. The Kings' Messengers, an organization supporting Church of England missions overseas, flourished in the village. It involved children and encouraged them to make useful items of sewing or knitting which would, under supervision, be of use to mission schools overseas. Where possible, a meeting would adopt a particular missionary or area.

In our village the choice was easy. A young man named Eddie Curtis, the eldest of five children of the innkeeper of the Stalbridge Arms had won a scholarship to Fosters School, Sherborne, in the 1920's. He had gone from there to Imperial College, London, where he took a chemistry degree and began teaching. He then decided to offer himself for ordination and become a missionary. He sailed for Mauritius and his school, he wrote home, needed simple bedspreads. So now our group had its own missionary and tremendous motivation.

The meetings were held after tea every week in the parish room across the road from our house. Bright cotton material was cut into squares and Jennie and I set to with a will to stitch them together. My stitches were dogs' teeth sized but no-one criticized and I enjoyed the work. Our cotton squares were of vivid, almost violent, red, blue, green and yellow which, we were assured, were what Mr. Curtis's children at the mission school liked best. I hope they did.

The grown-ups machined our strips together to make the bedspreads and they went to make up bales to be shipped out to the school. As we stitched, someone read out letters from Mr. Curtis about his work and the school. We studied a map on the wall to see where it was and learned quite a lot about the little island of Mauritius in the Indian Ocean. I was impressed. It all seemed such a remarkable thing to be doing in our Parish Room in the High Street.

Our year ended with Christmas and all the Church activities connected with it. Our rector was in touch with what was generally, if a little harshly, referred to as 'a slum parish' in one of the poorest parts of Jarrow, in the deeply depressed North of England, so every year, well before Christmas, we had a special service where we took presents up to the altar for them.

It was explained that the children of Jarrow lived in smoky streets lined with overcrowded houses. Everyone worked in factories, and there was nowhere to play except in the grimy streets. It sounded terrible. We had a factory in the street in our village but it was a milk factory. Jennie's relations connected with the factory would take us in there sometimes and give us mugs of ice cold milk and strips of milk powder warm off the rollers. I was quite sure the children of Jarrow would not get this sort of treatment from their factories, and no green fields either. My young heart ached.

At school as Christmas drew near we practised our carols for the school service in Church and for all the other services where carols seemed to replace the familiar hymns. One Christmas, while we were still living at Thornhill, 'Oh little Town of Bethlehem' became popular. My mother loved it. She bought the sheet music and she and Mary sang it about the house all that Christmas.

One of our best loved carols was 'Christians Awake' Our village blacksmith was named Christopher Jeans, known as Chris, and Jennie told me that the men and boys in the choir sometimes annoyed him by singing 'Chris Jeans Awake' outside his house. We thought this very funny indeed so we always sang that version ourselves.

We had a service just before Christmas for the dedication of the crib. One old flat tombstone in the Church was occupied by the cadaver effigy but the flat stone surface of another one near the altar was perfect for the crib – the same figures, kings, shepherds, fat sheep and contented looking cows, all worshipping the baby Jesus.

There was one church activity which could occur at any season. It was weddings, though most often in spring or summer. Several times in the year we would go up the steep hill 'to see a wedding come out'. This was always an excitement. Women and children would gather opposite the church's main door, the brides of the previous year, often with small babies in prams now, remarking: 'They're having our wedding hymn.' Then with a tremendous flourish on the rather fine organ, the bride and bridegroom appeared.

One fine August day I watched fascinated as a red carpet was laid from the Church door right across the hill to the front door of the doctor's house opposite. Our doctor's only daughter was to be married to a naval officer. The bride came out, the church bells pealed and all the waiting crowd seemed to be throwing confetti. That was in 1938. The next year brought war and many changes to the village and widowhood to the naval bride.

*   *   *   *   *

Our young lives were made full by church activities but mine was made even fuller by my family's involvement in the Congregational Chapel. There had by tradition been a Congregational meeting since 1662 and in 1724 a licence was granted for services to be held in a newly built meeting house in the village. The present chapel was built in 1870.

Members of my father's family supported it energetically.

His sisters, Kate and Annie, had been Sunday School teachers there, Kate until her marriage in 1909 and Annie until her untimely death in 1913. Kate had decided to marry a local man, a widower who was a builder on the outskirts of North London where he was thriving. In 1907 her father, Henry Rabbetts, had died and my aunt was of course very useful at home. Some of her family opposed the match and, such was the importance attached to the influence of the Congregational Chapel, they sent the minister to see her and try to persuade not to make the marriage.

Auntie Kate told me years later that she was in the garden at Cooks Farm when the Minister arrived by bicycle from Stalbridge. She was a quiet, shy woman but this time she spoke out

'Mr. Rose, I know why you've come but it's no good. I've made my bed. I've made it from the best feathers from my father's ducks and I can't waste it, so I'm going to be married.'

'Very well, my dear, I can see your mind's made up so I wish you well,' said the minister. And with that he mounted his bicycle and rode back to Stalbridge.

The chapel was well built and heated by an immense cast iron tortoise stove. The congregation wore their Sunday best clothes, often black or dark navy blue, and the heat from the stove seemed to bring out the scent of the mothballs that had preserved the clothes all the week. This was tempered by the smell of traditional Eau-de-Cologne – a lovely mixture to a child with a sharp nose.

On Sunday mornings I would go with my father to the morning service at 11 o'clock. At chapel, I soon realized, everybody joined in. The hymns were all easy to sing and everyone sang heartily. There was a special address for the children in the middle of the service, before they went out, then a sermon for the adults at the end.

I did not go out with the Chapel children so sat with my father through the sermon. Some were so long I started fidgeting, finally asking my father the time. He would solemnly draw his gold half hunter watch with its blue Roman figures from his pocket and silently show it to me. The watch was an impressive sight but some instinct warned me not to ask him the time again. My father was a naturally devout man and he listened carefully to the sermon.

When we came out my father exchanged greetings with fellow worshippers and I would trace the letters on the two gravestones in the tiny churchyard to the right of the Chapel's main door. One gravestone had the same name as ours and was erected, I knew, to my great-grandparents, George and Hester Rabbetts. The other bore the name of the Rev. Antonio Bisenti. Bisenti? Not surely an English name?

Years later I discovered that Mr. Bisenti was Portuguese by birth, born there in 1800. His parents had been killed in the Peninsular War against Napoleon and the boy fell in with some British soldiers at a camp commanded by the Duke of Wellington. A British officer befriended the orphaned Portuguese boy and brought him to England, where he was educated and put to business at Bath. In Bath he joined the congregation of the Vineyard's Chapel and began to preach in the villages around the city.

Eventually, Antonio Bisenti was ordained as a Congregational Minister and came to Stalbridge as pastor in 1833. He remained there until his death in 1872, visiting the poor and sick, attending the Parish Church on occasions and greatly loved. He spent nearly forty happy years in our village after a childhood disturbed by Napoleon.

Behind the chapel there was a school room with a small stage at one end. My mother went to a women's meeting there every Wednesday called the Sisterhood. In the holidays my mother took me with her, to sit quietly during the talk and to shut my eyes tight during the prayers. Some members of the Sisterhood were enthusiastic entertainers, often singing solos and duets or reciting poems, so when the Christmas party came, there was an entertainment.

The Christmas I was five my mother decided that I should recite a verse at the party. She coached me with great effort all the week before but I was paralysed with shyness at the very thought of a public performance. Members of the Sisterhood performed and were applauded. Perhaps I should be overlooked. But no, the minister, kind Mr. Lamb, said gently, 'I think we have another performance to come, haven't we?' There was no hope. My mother had told him. I shot out into the middle of the room and gabbled:

'To bed, to bed, said Sleepy Head
Tarry awhile, said Slow
Put on the pan said Greedy Nan
We'll sup before we go.'

The Sisterhood clapped most kindly and I hid my face in my mother's skirt. Meetings generally ended with a cup of tea and biscuits but at Christmas there was a gala tea and somebody brought seed cake. It was absolutely glorious, stuffed full of caraway seeds and light as a feather.

The small stage was invaluable for plays, children's concerts, entertainments and Harvest Festival concerts. For these anyone who could sing or recite, whether Church, Chapel, undenominational, Guides and Scouts or anything else, gave enjoyment to what was always a full house.

We also had a connection with the little mission chapel at Stalbridge Weston, a good country mile away. This chapel, stoutly built of rustless corrugated iron, was warm and friendly and behind the pulpit there was a large framed picture of my grandfather, Henry Rabbetts, just as we had at home. My grandfather, realising the need for a Congregational Chapel at Weston, had been the driving force behind collecting money and getting it built, early in the century.

Every year, as part of the Harvest Festival celebrations at the Weston chapel, the harvest produce was auctioned and my father was asked to be the auctioneer. He did this efficiently and cheerfully, using a small ornate wooden gavel kept for the purpose and I was very impressed when he took a bid from me for a bunch of carrots.

In 1938 my mother volunteered to become local secretary of the British and Foreign Bible Society when Miss Stella Prideaux, the daughter of the owner of the milk factory, married and moved away. This activity united Church and Chapel, since members of both were happy to subscribe towards the provision of bibles in the vernacular throughout the world. Most of the new secretary's work for the Bible Society was the collection of subscriptions. Many had to be collected from outlying farms and the Annual General Meeting was approaching. Mr. Prideaux came to the rescue and provided a car and driver to enable my mother to collect the money, taking me with her. A car and a driver! If this was working for the Bible Society I was going to enjoy it. But, as soon as I was considered safe on a bicycle, collecting subscriptions from remote farm houses, often several miles from home and down muddy cart tracks, became my job. I still enjoyed it though, for the farmers' wives did not see many visitors and made me very welcome in their warm farm kitchens.

My parents belonged to different denominations and by definition to different political parties, but they had agreed when they married that in their house there should never be any argument about these topics or criticism of their positions. There never was and, more than that, my father consented to our Church of England upbringing and my mother worked hard for any cause that would bring Church and Chapel together. When she died the Rector of the time said at her funeral, 'She was the ecumenical movement personified.'

10

Our World and Beyond

IN MANY WAYS Stalbridge in the 1930's was an enclosed world and my childhood was happily enclosed within it. Some social and religious customs were unchanged, as if we were still living in a late medieval society or where the upheavals of the Reformation were so thoroughly absorbed that we did not notice them.

Generations of acute shortage of money in this secluded place had bred instinctive thrift and the ingrained conviction that it was morally wrong to spend money on oneself. So clothes of hardwearing serge, tweed and leather, cherished carefully and reserved for Sundays, lasted well. Old ladies in Chapel on Sundays might still wear Edwardian servant girls' elastic-sided boots with their long dark skirts and coats, and black hats skewered with jet tipped hatpins into a grey bun. As the tortoise stove warmed up the chapel in winter the smell of mothballs from the clothes of the congregation hung in the air.

Attractive styles of former years could still be seen. Lace on heirloom collars and jabots relieved the general darkness of clothes with great effect. Old Mrs. Hobbs, from the tailors shop in the High Street, wore lovely lace collars, and with her white hair piled up and set off with combs, she looked a picture. An inky black or deep mauve velvet ribbon was sometimes threaded through a mother-of-pearl heirloom buckle and worn high up against the throat.

The fiercely bobbed hair and short skirts that followed the Great War had gone now. Hair was given a fearsome four hour permanent wave – a 'perm'- which produced a harsh frizzled finish and, when set, rows of stiff curls. Mary and her friends preferred the fashionable marcel wave, which was softer and more elegant.

Elegance permeated the mid-Thirties scene. Trousers for women, wide and often called beach pyjamas, had become acceptable and smart. Auntie Millie had parted from her first husband and gone to London as a fashion buyer, so naturally she had some wide-legged trousers. In a snapshot of her in Brighton in these, she looked extremely smart. This fashion did not reach Stalbridge but we did sometimes see tennis dresses with wide-legged divided skirts or, now that rambling and cycling in groups had become popular, girls in shorts.

Standard wear for business girls at Graces the drapers was a simple black dress. They managed to enliven it with a light collar, brooches or necklaces so that they did not look as if they were wearing a uniform. The hours of shop assistants were long and the work hard. In a time of Depression like this, there was little job security and dismissal could be instant. After work, though, there could be dancing.

Harry James the trumpeter, and band leaders Ambrose, Joe Loss and Jimmy Dorsey were all established in this period and became famous later. All these big bands still capture for me the essence of my childhood, but the one I liked most was Victor Silvester whose orchestra was famous for its strict tempo. Local dance bands played this kind of music and the big bands made records. There were many evenings when the business girls threw off their black dresses for something more colourful and danced.

Babies wore white, often swathed in beautiful hard-knitted shawls. To see a young baby in the white interior of a huge baby-carriage pram of those days was like looking into a white cave.

My abiding memory of my own clothes concerns a green velvet party dress with a white lace collar. Auntie Millie had sent it with special party knickers, more abbreviated than usual. Sometimes we went to tea with people who still had horsehair chairs and sofas in the best room. I had to sit still so the only occupation I could think of was to wriggle round and study the many sepia photographs. The rasping of rough cold horsehair against the tops of my bare legs makes me shudder still.

Rather surprisingly perhaps, fur collars were everywhere, either as a trimming to a garment or a cape for children or as a free standing fur which had obviously begun life on some thin brown animal with hard, beady little eyes. What sort of animal I would wonder in Chapel stank of mothballs? Later in the Thirties fox furs might be seen in the village, the head apparently biting the tail.

Beige, with fawn and brown, seemed to be everywhere – on clothes, carpets, curtains and fireplaces – sometimes softened with cream or enlivened with patches of bright yellow, orange or scarlet stylised flowers. In our house we had red poppies sprawling over pale cream tea cups, a design almost jazzy enough to make me enjoy washing up.

The most astonishing result of these popular designs was my mother's bridge coat, a fashionable garment of the period. She did not play bridge (though she and my father taught us to play whist once they found we could concentrate enough to avoid trumping our partner's ace) and the coat had once belonged to Mrs. Medlycott of Venn House, near Milborne Port. It was made of black panne velvet, with a pattern of stylised scarlet poppies picked out in gold lame thread on the fronts.

My mother rarely went out in the evening, except to choral society practice or a meeting connected with church or chapel. However, occasionally something would happen to justify her wearing the bridge coat and I loved its soft slithery feel.

Clothes for men in this farming community had to be hard wearing and protect the wearer from the weather, so leather, tweed, corduroy and flannel abounded, with whipcord for riding breeches. Boots for work were preserved with dubbin, a black grease that could never produce a shine.

Overalls, blue, brown or possibly green, of hard wearing denim, were often worn over trousers. Clothes were protected according to the work done by the wearer. The baker who delivered bread wore a sturdy enveloping brown denim coat, rather like a brown version of the modern white lab coat. The two butchers wore either striped butchers' aprons or the same sort of brown coat (or both), and girls who worked in Dikes were issued with brown or green coat-like overalls.

Bakers' or grocers' assistants who handled food and did not expect to get messy, wore white aprons, and great care was taken to see that the apron was always spotlessly clean.

On Sundays a man who wore a suit to Church or Chapel usually wore it for a long country walk in the afternoon. My father, who firmly believed that the best is cheapest in the end, bought a mid-brown suit of such good quality that I never remember him wearing anything else on Sundays. He added a brown trilby hat, brushed his suit and hat carefully, adding (perhaps surprisingly) a ready made bow tie to his shirt and, thus prepared, set out for Chapel. It was his invariable routine.

We in this quiet place were sometimes made aware of the world outside the village. In 1929 a firm of prospectors for oil came to Hewletts Farm and my father allowed them to make test bores. My mother remembered for years how the man in charge wore a frock coat and top hat on the farm, which she felt was overdoing it. They did not find oil and I think my parents were relieved, but if they had, the nearness of the railway would have made the site ideal.

The railway, the Somerset and Dorset Joint Railway from Bath to Bournemouth had been established in 1874.When we lived at Hewletts Farm the trains, some sixteen a day, ran through the Home Ground and were so reliable you could set your watch by them, and I often heard my parents recall the eerie quiet that descended on the farm during the General Strike in 1926 when no trains ran.

The railway gave us cheap day excursion tickets to the seaside and an important express train, the Pines Express, ran from Bournemouth to the Midlands, but for some extraordinary reason stopped at Stalbridge. This meant that on our rare visits to our relations in Gloucester we could go straight there on the express.

The cinema brought the big world to us. As well as our Monday night travelling cinema we had the Odeon Cinema at Yeovil, a lovely classic white cinema set in pretty public gardens. Here they showed 'Gone With the Wind', surely the most hyped up film ever made. It featured Vivien Leigh, a beauty whose first husband had been a Wiltshireman, but more important to my mother, Leslie Howard, an archetypical English film star whom she greatly admired, was in the film. It lasted for four hours, too long, it was decided, for me , but one day I went with her to see 'Pimpernel Smith' in which Leslie Howard spirited political prisoners out of the new concentration camps of Nazi Germany. The plot was a bit lost on me, but I thought my mother looked grave.

Miss Pearse kept us abreast of current affairs. Once, with her customary dramatic flair, she told us about the plight of little dark-eyed children, helpless before waves of bombing in a place with an unpronounceable name in Spain. The Spanish Civil War had broken out and the town was Guernica.

Towards the end of 1936 I became aware that my parents were preoccupied about something. Occasionally, I would come into the room and hear them discussing 'that woman,' then seeing me they changed the subject. I was naturally immensely interested in all this and turned over in my mind who 'that woman' could be. It must be someone in our village and someone who was 'fast', so I supposed she wore rouge like a circus clown and mascara that clogged her eyelashes together. I went through the candidates (there were not many) but could not think of anyone who could so seriously annoy my parents by her behaviour.

Then it was December and Miss Pearse told us firmly that we must not on any account sing the version of 'Hark the Herald Angels Sing' that went:

'Hark the herald angels sing,
Mrs. Simpson stole our King'

and the mystery was explained. My parents considered Edward VIII's Abdication and subsequent marriage to the twice-divorced Mrs. Simpson to be a scandalous dereliction of duty and were appalled by it. The Abdication did, however, give us a new king with a pretty, lively wife and two little girls, one older and one younger than me.

On 6th May, 1937, the new King provided us with the excitement of his Coronation. Stalbridge High Street was enveloped in flags and bunting. My parents borrowed two enormous Union flags on poles and hung them out of the bedroom windows.

We had no wireless, but on Coronation Day we were invited to listen to the service on the wireless of Mrs. Chappell, who lived in a bungalow at the end of the village. Mrs. Chappell looked after her husband and his father. Her father-in-law was sprightly and active but her husband had been severely gassed in the First World War. He was a shadow of a man, a thin, clenched figure in a wheelchair. He did not speak and I was not sure whether he could hear. He wore dark glasses behind which he appeared to have very little sight. We were grouped around the wireless. I was put on a low chair with Mr. Chappell in his wheelchair beside me. We all listened intently, it was such a new experience, and in the quiet parts of the service I was aware of Mr. Chappell's laboured breathing. Shortly after the Coronation the Chappell family left the village, and before long we heard that the invalid had died.

The horrors of the Great War had bound the survivors together. This comradeship, so poignant on Armistice Sunday when ex-servicemen paraded quietly along the village street past grave-faced onlookers, continued. A branch of the British

Legion had been founded after the war, using an old army hut until the Branch was able to build its own premises in 1932. The Hut then became the social centre of the entire village, while the Great War Comrades flourished in The Legion on Barrow Hill and their summer outings to the seaside in Lovelace's or Seager's 'Sharry' were annual features.

Sometimes news of the world outside reached us through my mother's work for the British and Foreign Bible Society. She had become secretary and treasurer of our branch. The Annual General Meeting, presided over by the Rector with the Congregational and Methodist Ministers loyally supporting him, was addressed by a speaker from the Society. One year, to my great delight, the speaker told us how there had been a tremendous increase in the sale of small pocket bibles on fine paper in a mountainous region of Yugoslavia. The Society at first rejoiced, then became suspicious and a staff member was sent out to discover what had caused the sudden upsurge of these purchases. They found there was brisk trade in smuggling tobacco through the mountains and the pages of the bibles provided excellent paper for rolling cigarettes.

Politics did not impinge much on my family's lives. My father was as unshakeable in his Liberal as in his nonconformist convictions. He therefore supported free trade in deference to the one and total abstinence from intoxicating liquor in deference to the other. Years later I was glad to realize that my father never knew that H.H. Asquith, whom he greatly admired, drank intoxicating liquor with enthusiasm.

My mother's low church Anglicanism was combined with an instinctive preference for the Conservative party. She felt it an excellent thing that society should be ordered, that people should know their place and work hard to look out for themselves. No-one, though, could have given more practical help and sympathy to the underdog and the unfortunate.

In our local constituency of North Dorset the Conservative candidate, Sir Charles Hanbury, won the election in 1935. The

Hon. W. Borthwick stood for the Liberal party, Miss M. Whitehead stood for Labour and, significantly, George Pitt-Rivers, a local squire, stood for the North Dorset Agricultural Defence League. I cannot help wondering if my parents voted for him this time, but somehow, I doubt it. Within two years of this election Sir Charles Hanbury died and there was a by-election.

This time there were only two candidates. The Conservative was Captain Angus Valdimar Hambro, a magistrate and President of the Society of Dorset Men for many years. The other, the Liberal candidate, was the Hon. W. Borthwick, and I soon lost interest when Captain Hambro won the seat.

In April 1937 an aircraft carrier, the *Ark Royal*, was launched and later that year we saw it. We were in Weymouth, either on an outing or during my father's convalescence there and the *Ark Royal* could be seen out in Weymouth Bay. Someone told us the name of the ship. It was so topical and we gazed fascinated as she gleamed peacefully in the sunshine. Then I ran down the sands and into the sea. The Second World War would come one day and alter our lives for ever, but it had not come yet.

Epilogue

THESE YEARS that I have described – where did they all lead? I had grown up in the happy world of the village and the village school where change was slow and slight. It was a world bounded by the seasons, where strangers were an event that caused heads to turn and speculation to be made, a world where we all knew each other and, in many ways, cared for each other.

It was a time where for me lifelong friendships were forged. Jennie I have remained devoted to, and in the period I have described, two other lifelong friendships began. The first was with a boy named Mervyn whose widowed mother had taken work on a farm just outside the village. Mervyn had spent a long time in hospital and his mother now wanted him to live near her. My mother heard of the situation and Mervyn came to live with us. He was gentle and quiet and not in the least like the dreaded boys at school. We would take our jam jars and fish for tadpoles and minnows in cow ponds and streams that always seemed extraordinarily well stocked. We have remained the best of friends ever since and his son is my godchild.

The other friendship forged in those pre-war days was with Kathleen, a girl slightly younger than me, who was born and brought up on the next farm to ours. Our mothers were friends. Our elder sisters were good friends in the same class at school, a friendship which endured throughout their lives. The result was that Kathleen and I 'inherited' each other, remaining good friends and, since middle age, travelling the world together.

The stable friendships I was lucky enough to make then were a boon, for change was coming to our seemingly changeless little world. Neville Chamberlain flew to Munich in 1938 and came back with a worthless peace of paper and a year for Britain to buy time and re-arm.

After war was declared in September 1939 change came with a vengeance. Soldiers of the King's Royal Rifle Corps were stationed in Stalbridge. Many were billeted in the village and our little sitting room was commandeered to take pairs of them. A large, impressive officer came to make the arrangement. When my mother explained that she hadn't enough beds, the officer roared:

'Beds, Madam, beds! This is war. My men will sleep on the floor.'

Evacuees came to the Junior School. It was no longer our school for Jennie and I had gone up the year before to the Senior School beyond the Church, where we were in Standard IV, the lowest standard, and where the head teacher Mr. Trewhella was another good teacher and forceful personality. The Junior School was being used as a reception centre for evacuees from the East End of London. They were pale and sallow with Cockney voices that to our ears sounded shrill. Jennie and I, looking through the railings of the school playground, realized with a start that some of the women had hair of a deep, dense shade of red, such as we'd never seen on a human head before. It was, my mother explained later when we asked her about it, henna that made it that colour. Their hair was dyed! For once, my mother did not equate this with being 'fast' – I suppose because it was now wartime.

By our country standards some of the children, especially boys of ten or eleven, were undersized for their age. My mother decided that this may well have been the result of poor nutrition but, she added firmly, 'They've probably been smoking on the quiet for years.'

The war made my mother extremely busy. She had never been

afraid of hard work and the pressure on her to feed and accommodate the many people who came to our door needing somewhere to stay, was intense. In addition to all this she found time to attend a series of daytime Red Cross lectures. These were extremely practical, embracing the action to be taken in dire emergencies – conditions we daily expected.

An old lady of well over ninety came and, when a patient was required to be bandaged, treated for shock and loaded on to a stretcher, she volunteered. She made an excellent patient for she was soon sound asleep.

My mother was constantly asked to take in the family members of soldiers stationed in the village. On one occasion the doting mother of a sergeant came for a few days and, as her son had leave, he also stayed. Sergeant he may have been, but we were quietly delighted at breakfast when his mother cut the top off his boiled egg, saying proudly,

'Just as I always have, you see, ever since he was a little boy.'

Early in 1940 a young rifleman in the King's Royal Rifle Corps asked my mother if she could accommodate his wife for a bit to get her away from London and spend time with him before he was posted, very probably overseas. The girl came, a nervous eighteen-year-old. In June her husband was killed at the battle for Calais and the young wife, by then expecting a baby, stayed on with us. Eventually, the baby was born in our house. The little boy was delivered by our much respected Dr. Moyle, my mother being the midwife. After Dr. Moyle had made his first visit on the day of the birth, and arranged to come again later, he asked if he could leave his black bag at the house. My mother took him into our 'best' front room saying, 'It will be quite safe there, Doctor,'

'Oh good,' he replied gravely. 'It's got the baby in it.'

The baby was born shortly after ten o'clock that night and Doctor Moyle left our house as the customers were leaving the Swan Hotel opposite. They bombarded him with enquiries and good wishes which the young mother, who heard them, never forgot.

The summer of 1940 must have been a desperately anxious time for all the grownups in the village. Once, my mother met Leslie Hobbs standing outside his tailor's shop in the High Street. They stood and watched as the sky went black above them with German bombers heading for Bristol. Leslie's face was grey.

'What chance have we got?' He said quietly.

My mother did not tell anyone about this conversation until after the Battle of Britain had been fought and won.

The Local Defence Volunteers, later the Home Guard, were being recruited and trained. Local men became volunteer firemen or Air Raid Wardens and strict blackout regulations were enforced. Meaders, our hardware shop, sold rolls of dense blackout material, as any window showing a light at night could have drawn the attention of German bombers overhead. My father always drew our blackout curtains himself, not allowing anyone to go upstairs until he had done so.

In the beautiful summer of 1940, after France had fallen and the heroic evacuation of Dunkirk had been completed, the German army was daily expected to invade somewhere along the Dorset coast. Weymouth Bay was doubly barricaded with heavy iron structures, tank traps were laid and pill boxes set up at vulnerable places on roads and railways. Signposts and place names were hastily removed so that the invaders might not know where they were. Careful instructions were broadcast on the wireless telling people what to do in the event of an enemy invasion.

One afternoon, I found my mother quietly packing a suitcase.

'What are you doing?' I asked.

She replied gently, 'We might have to leave this house and go and live in the woods for a bit, so I'm packing some food for us to take.'

This sounded very interesting and novel. Then I remembered my beloved teddy bear.

'I'm not going without Teddy,' I said.

'All right dear. Sit him on the suitcase. Then we shan't forget to take him.'

Teddy sat on the suitcase all through that long, hot summer, a beloved symbol of the happy home and ordered childhood I had known before the war.